More Than Watchmen At Daybreak

poems by Cyrus Cassells

Also by Cyrus Cassells

The Mud Actor (1982)
Soul Make a Path through Shouting (1994)
Beautiful Signor (1997)
More Than Peace and Cypresses (2004)
The Crossed-Out Swastika (2012)
The Gospel according to Wild Indigo (2018)
The World That The Shooter Left Us (2022)
Is There Room For Another Horse on Your Horse Ranch? (2024)

Translations

Still Life With Children: Selected Poems of Francesc Parcerisas (2019)

NINE MILE BOOKS

Publisher: Nine Mile Art Corp.
Editors: Bob Herz, Stephen Kuusisto, Andrea Scarpino
Art Editor Emeritus: Whitney Daniels
Cover Art: Flock 2 by Julie Whyman

Nine Mile Books is an imprint of Nine Mile Art Corp

The publishers gratefully acknowledge support of the New York State Council on the Arts with the support of Governor Andrew M. Cuomo and the New York State Legislature. We also acknowledge support of the County of Onondaga and CNY Arts through the Tier Three Project Support Grant Program. We have also received significant support from the Central New York Community Foundation. This publication would not have been possible without the generous support of these groups. We are very grateful to them all.

ISBN: 978-1-7326600-7-6

ACKNOWLEDGMENTS

Many thanks to the Benedictine Brothers of the Christ in the Desert Monastery, the Fine Arts Work Center in Provincetown, the Mabel Dodge Foundation, and to Texas State University for their support.

"Mary's Day" is for Kathleen Peirce.

These poems first appeared in the following magazines, some in earlier versions: *Agni*: "More Than Watchmen at Daybreak"; *Green Mountains Review*: "Oh The Snow is a Blinding Sight to See"; *Nine Mile*: "Accepting the Peace of Saint Francis Hermitage," "Celestial Prayers," "Diary of a Pentecost Sunday," "Monastic Silence," "A Monk's Textbook of Shadows," "Winter Abbey With Venus Rising"; *The Southampton Review*: "Cool and Living Like a March Branch," "Mary's Day," and "Messengers of the Desert Air."

Many thanks to Veronica Golos for her help with finding the cover art.

CONTENTS

Author's Note

I. Winter Abbey with Venus Rising

II. Accepting the Peace of Saint Francis Hermitage

III. Lighting *Farolitos* on a Windy Christmas Eve

IV. Messengers of the Desert Air

V. Oh The Snow Is a Blinding Sight To See

VI. Cool and Living Like a March Branch

VII. Mary's Day

VIII. Monastic Silence

IX. A Monk's Textbook of Shadows

X. Celestial Prayers

XI. Diary of a Pentecost Sunday

XII. More Than Watchmen at Daybreak

About Cyrus Cassells

Author's Note

In 2018, the prior and Benedictine brothers of Christ in the Desert Monastery in Abiquiu, New Mexico, gifted me with two hermitages to use for my writing. The first was on Three Kings Day in January at the Peace of Saint Francis Hermitage, close to the novice's quarters, and the second was in May, August, and December at the Saint Augustan of Canterbury Hermitage, next to the Chama River—a fifteen-minute walk from the monastery's striking chapel and main grounds. There was no Internet or phone reception. It was the first time in my life I was incommunicado for a long stretch and the results were dramatic. I've been composing new poetry and cultural criticism nonstop since the first wintry day that I landed in Abiquiu.

This twelve-part sequence, "More Than Watchmen at Daybreak," examines the immense natural beauty of the abbey's Chama Valley setting, with its red and saffron-yellow cliffs, and the devotional life and hardy activities of the monks. The title is biblical:

> *More than watchmen at daybreak,*
> *My soul is longing for the Lord*

Psalm 130:6

More Than Watchmen At Daybreak

I.   Winter Abbey
      with Venus Rising

Pilgrim, under in-a-rush chevrons
Of restless desert clouds,

At shape-shifting winter's onset,
Picture the Benedictines' elating valley,

Its eminent gusts yielding
A Yuletide jackpot of curt,

Valedictory leaves—whirling, marshaling
In windswept cardinal directions:

Broadcast realm of *glory be*, insurgent
Kingdom of *kyrie eleison*—

Solstice: a slowly ascending,
Bold as a horseman sun

Burnishes each antediluvian cliff,
Each telltale winter crest,

With its equalizing gaze:
A resolute, dispassionate topaz—

Far from the deriding republic,
A mint-new Herod's decrees,

The poignant bronze of reed beds,
The strict rhythm of the liturgical hours,

And later, as irrepressible Venus rises,
Consecrating the far-flung abbey,

And the stalwart compass star appears,
The ink of darkened, sacramental banks

With pallid embroideries of ice,
The blessed Jerusalem of the pewter river—

II. Accepting the Peace
of Saint Francis Hermitage

Listen, out of love and goodwill,
I was given a hermitage—

From the prior's hand, a choir stall
Of layered terracotta cliffs to contemplate,

To venerate: *Benedictus qui venit*
In nomine domini,

Benedictus qui venit . . .
A cusp of inchoate vermilion

And liberating blue,
An umber ribbon-length, imagine,

Of rustic, unpaved road,
Ushering my winter-proof boots

Past grazing ruminants and the lissome river's
Glitter and meander—

Dear beneficent prior,
Will I find impartial God

In the timeworn mountains that cradle
Cassiopeia and Cygnus, The Great Swan?

Will I learn to embrace the wind-blessed
Peace and serenity of Saint Francis?

In the breeze-plied December abbey,
Under the Dipper seeker,

Each midnight now I'm seized
By the imperial Milky Way,

The mainstay Seven Sisters,
Ruby-rare ornaments,

Gleaming in the brisk black cauldron
Of the midnight river's buffeted mirror—

III. Lighting *Farolitos* on a Windy Christmas Eve

On a pell-mell Christmas Eve,
Whistling, planning Brother Dorian has crafted

A poignant crèche
From malleable mud and cut-away timber—

Though a hectoring canyon wind
Defies us, bedevils us,

After a dogged, wintry dusk,
The desert abbey is adorned at last

By lucent rows of Southwestern *farolitos*,
Italicizing the exacting (yet utterly elating!) task

Of our chilly sundown handiwork,
We, intent seekers who represent

The earth's diverse stations
(Malawi, Quebec, Poland, Vietnam...)

Questing strangers,
Yuletide pilgrims who've assembled:

Mabel, who's battling liver cancer,
Victor-Emanuel, who's sponsoring a school in Lima

For eager children to bloom
Into sterling thinkers and prescient leaders,

Cameron, who has veered far from home
Since his querulous wife revealed

She's pregnant by his closest friend:
City-dwelling dreamer, desperate

As a foraging Joseph
Seeking an eligible inn and finding

Only a dismaying manger—

Now almost hallowing snowflakes settle
On still-irate Cam's dynamic shoulders

Like delicate epaulettes:
May he (may each of us) embrace

Suffusing peace or enduring truce
In this desert canyon at Christmas.

IV. Messengers of the Desert Air

If, in the enveloping morning, new disciple,
In the messiah's desert garden, I sing

Kestrel's caw, golden eagle's arc, hawk's reconnoiter,
Remember, here in this arid valley,

The myriad raptors,
Agile ravens, and go-for-broke jays

Can, in a match-stroke, be revealed
As daylight messengers;

If I declare *January's lamp-black banner,*
A flag of rallying crows,

It might mean the traveling Benedictine
With his indispensible staff,

His windswept sleeves, billowing,
Black as a king's cortege,

All at once halting on the uphill road

To salute you, noontime apostle—
Avid and long-blessed,

So full of stamina,
You who have idolized

The sibylline birds,
The spinning earth's pine-green allure,

But have been, in your marrowbones,
A benighted foreigner

To reverential stillness
And pressing, altering silence,

A stranger (deaf as Beethoven at the close)
To unutterable beauty—

V. Oh The Snow Is
A Blinding Sight To See

A mint-new snowfall has subsumed
The last hints of gold and healing russet

From the ambushed fields,
And, look, the brindled roan,

Alarmed or truant—
Untellable from this distance—

Canters down
The white-clad canyon path

(Pale as a linen corporal
Sewn for a communion chalice)

Past the Benedictine abbey's curl
Of piñon smoke, and the marble swirl

Of the winter-stilled river,
Transiting from the magical

Twelfth day of Christmas to attain
The kingdom of Ordinary Time,

And for a perishable hour, the regnant moon
Takes our monkish longings,

Our makeshift and human prayers
Back into her weightless,

Voluminous light,
The way a snow fox proffers

Its almost blinding fur . . .

VI. Cool and Living
Like a March Branch

When the green of the canyon river returns,
The subtle celadon and silver,

And the match-burst glory of the altar's
Flush, conspicuous poinsettias

Becomes a far-off memory,
Then I'm finally ready

For the specter of Christ's surrender,
For the sure-footed donkey

And inspiriting palms,
Cast down in praise of the far-seeing Nazarene—

Now, after a releasing wolf's hour rain,
Come fragrant paroxysms of sage,

Clandestine swatches of melting ice
In little declensions—

Thawing winter: oh let me love again
The woodpecker's artistry,

A noisy quorum of geese
Abruptly lifting from the gilded

Surface of the fluent Chama,
Flecked with giveaway islets of foam—

At accumulating dusk, the cliff's shadow
Visible in the untrammeled current,

Hungry mallards voluble all at once,
In concert with the healing call to vespers—

VII. Mary's Day

Wait! This hour of circling kestrels
And callous sentries' dice,

This rain-undoing Friday
Of unremitting nails—

Clarified by mordant daylight
And searing torchlight,

Hear me out,
Is also Mary's day:

Mary the mourner,
The peerless maker, the harrowed

Witness to her son's
Desecrated body, human majesty

That can never be recovered,
Not by hyssop or unceasing prayer—

Mary the fearless, intent listener,
Forever bending to gauge

The tenor of her small son's cough—

VIII. Monastic Silence

Listen to the unstoppable Chama's
Roaring missive,

The arresting hawk's cry,
The clanging bell at starry vigils—

Then sere, demanding
Ghost town in the Wild West silence—

Deep as a dilapidated well,
Door-closing silence—

The vast scapular,
The sable cloak of night—

Clapper-less silence:
Monk's paramour,

Soul's rosary,
Saint's reliable stratagem—

Here comes the rallying cry of the wild,
Spinning weathervane,

The canyon storm's alarum,
Quick, harridan-harsh rain claiming

A deep-carved arroyo,
Then sheriff-fierce,

Swift-footed silence,
The see-no-evil,

Hear-no-evil,
Speak-no-evil denouement,

The red desert *deus ex machina,*
The tight-lipped auto-da-fé—

Silence, immense silence,
Surpassing all human design,

Bellowing silence.

IX. A Monk's Textbook
of Shadows

Brother Lucien, in the roaring hush
That seizes your austere cell,

You imagine that you hear
The busybody world's rampant demons;

Well, I've got your demons:
Truth-teller, God-seeker, listen,

As a diligent pupil, you don't have to study
Break-spirit lynching trees

Or the Trail of Tears
(Foot sores and fever blankets,

Swamps and insolvent treaties...) to quail
At the long, abominable spell

Of inglorious shadow,
At the brutish deputy in us,

The lack-love warrior who clamors
For the spilled blood of others

And heralds it as new-pressed wine—

X. Celestial Prayers

As Christ in his desert crucible
Became brother to the limitless, starry sky,

There's never a lucent night
In the outlying hermitage

When I'm not a loyal son
Or a half-besotted cousin

To all-centering Polaris,
Watch-me-everybody Sirius, and The Northern Cross—

Listen, on my tenth birthday, I was taught,
By my assiduous pilot father,

The sundial's impetus,
The red-hot equator's pivotal role,

And the passkey beauty
Of springtime constellations—

In the cricket-praised valley,
Where witching hour or wolf's hour

Clarity is the reigning king,
Sometimes I dream

Of opening my mendicant mouth
(Delicate as a gilded carp's

Or a leaping dolphin's rictus),
And letting the unfailing night

Feed me its impossible provender
Of planets and prodigal stars,

Or keener, better, richer:
Bless me with celestial prayers.

XI. Diary of
a Pentecost Sunday

A brazen hummingbird's flurry,
Its side-swiping motor at my breath—

Ready-to-dazzle dragonflies spotted
Near the Saint Augustan hermitage,

And, all at once,
A quicksilver heron skimming

The fleet, mutable river's hem—

*

Comes Pentecost, with its leitmotif of fire
And rushing wind,

Of springtime babel
And cut-to-the heart communion—

Revealing unforgettable Christ's return
To his still-stunned disciples,

All believers, all witnesses
To the brutal cross

And to doleful, prostrate Mary—
Pentecost: a protean heat,

An earnest gust magically toppling
The myriad imposing barriers between

The manifold earth's competing languages—

*

On Pentecost morning,
I wake to four gadabout monastery horses,

Grazing and boldly neighing
Right below my bedroom sill;

Here's the mahogany force of Montana,
The most engaging roan;

As I leave the Saint Augustan of Canterbury hermitage
And lean over the adobe fence,

He gallantly poses, with his long, pert neck,
As if on command,

And lowers to accept
My May-time plum and Gala apple:

The warmth of my surrendering fingertips,
The fire of my own precipitous giving,

The cooling fruit, believer, unbeliever,
The word of a festive, luminous language—

*

At Pentecost mass, Father John cites
Thomas Merton's experience of oneness

In an unremarkable Kentucky mall,
And I recall my own such mystical moments

Occurred in a dusty train station anteroom
And in a bustling burger-and-fries diner,

When the vibrant strings of the logos,
The vast puppet master, began to shine,

And only untarnished connection,
Only abiding union was revealed—

Though most Sundays all we have on earth
Is subjectivity: this tensile,

Two-pronged language of duality,
This tattoo of I-and-Thou—

*

The pearl of communion means
For Mark, my longtime friend, a poet,

Three oracular horses in an unassuming field:
Fresh vision that ferried him back

To "the cold womb at the heart of nothing."

*

After the intricacies and rigors of mass,
I remembered the surprising tale

Of my former student,
Who polished the word glossolalia

And hailed from a busy, ardent
Pentecostal family,

Yet was queer, God of Abraham,
Queer and found it impossible

To ever speak in tongues—

*

Full spring: the once-spare desert valley
Costumed in voluble greens

And showboat yellows—
Now, suddenly, the nave blue,

Eggshell, and fork-silver palette
Of the invigorating sundown sky—

*

Everywhere spring's preponderant
Green flames, and now,

After satisfying Sunday vespers, the soft
"Peace be with you" of the first peony

That the black-robed prior plucks
And brings to me from the cloister garden.

XII. More Than Watchmen
at Daybreak

The river's soft pistons, the river's black silk
Under shooting stars—

The voluble ink and silver-white sky
Looming above the stark monastery

Becomes the coppice elk's vast eternity—
The duenna moon,

All at once coquettish,
Brash as sin, blanches

The river-curve, the heron,
The corral of fast-asleep horses—

August: the souls says,
Yes, I was there:

When raffish, runaway flames
Claimed the orphanage,

When rampant smoke drove the dying
Into the summer sea;

Present when riled protestors cried
If they fire into the crowd . . .

And then they fired into the crowd;
When the aghast stranger, fingering

A galling dungeon photo, asked,
What kind of God would allow *that?*—

More than fleet, querying owls,
More than nightlong watchmen,

Born wide-awake and dying, I confess
Not even this wondrous colossus

Of shooting stars,
The extravagant earth's countless beauties

Seem capable of quenching this lust,
This innermost hunger for return—

Incensed and restive
In this desert monastery,

Thirsty, fallible, but not yet resigned,
Full of questions and parrying,

Lord Buddha, God of Abraham,
From wolf's hour to blue hour

To burgeoning dawn—

About Cyrus Cassells

Cyrus Cassells's *The Gospel according to Wild Indigo* was a finalist for the 2018 Balcones Prize, the NAACP Image Award, and the Texas Institute of Letters Helen C. Smith Award. *Still Life with Children: Selected Poems of Francesc Parcerisas*, translated from the Catalan, was published in 2019. A current Guggenheim fellow, he has also won the National Poetry Series, a Lambda Literary Award, a Lannan Literary Award, a Pushcart Prize, and two NEA grants. His twin 7th and 8th books, *The World That the Shooter Left Us* (2022) and *Is There Room For Another Horse on Your Horse Ranch?* (2024) are forthcoming from Four Way Books.

Photo credit: Fabrizio Darold

Made in the USA
Middletown, DE
21 November 2025

22422937R00123

FAITH THAT TRANSFORMS
GOD'S POWER AND AUTHORITY UNLOCKED

ANTHONY VAUGHN

For additional information and booking, Contact Anthony Vaughn at
www.anthonyvaughnbooks.com

Faith that Transforms: God's Power and Authority Unlocked
ISBN: 979-8-218-65494-8
First Edition
Printed in the United States of America

This book is a work of inspiration and empowerment. While every effort has been made
to ensure accuracy, the information is provided "as is." The author and publisher shall not
be held liable for any damages resulting from the use of this material.

Dedication

With heartfelt gratitude and love, I dedicate this book to my amazing wife, Sharon. You are my rock, my confidant, and a strong tower of faith and resilience. Your unwavering belief in me and the calling God has placed on my life has been my greatest source of inspiration throughout this journey. You have been my greatest blessing, and a living reminder of God's unchanging faithfulness. Thank you for your unshakable support, for walking beside me through every challenge and triumph, and for being the embodiment of love and devotion. I am deeply grateful for your love and support, and I could not have done this without you. I am forever grateful for the gift of you.

To my brilliant and beloved children: Ramah, Chinara, Terron, and Armani, and my two cherished grandchildren: each of you are a radiant gift from God, a living testament to His grace and purpose. You fill my heart with indescribable joy and illuminate my life with your presence. Through your lives, you have taught me the true meaning of love, resilience, and unwavering faith, lessons that words could never fully express. You inspire me daily to live with intention and serve with love. I am eternally thankful for the beauty, strength, and legacy you bring into my life.

Acknowledgments

To my esteemed pastor of over 45 years, Bishop Walter S. Thomas, Sr.:

It is challenging to adequately convey the significant influence you have had on my life. Your spirit-filled teachings, your dynamic and relatable approach to sharing the Gospel of Jesus Christ, and your unwavering friendship have been a transformative force in shaping who I am today.

To my esteemed lifelong friend Elder Joseph Dodson, and friends Alvin Bagley and Ferly Yerby:

Your profound words of encouragement and ongoing support have been invaluable over the years.

Many thanks to Joyce Anderson for her invaluable assistance.

To my talented daughter, Chinara Smith:

Your contributions have been truly indispensable in bringing this book to life. Your passion, hard work, and commitment have not only elevated this vision but have also been a source of inspiration to me. I extend my sincere gratitude to you.

To my prayer warriors—Morris York, Algia Ford, and Reverend Mackey McLaughlin:

Your prayers and words of encouragement have been my lifeline. Your partnership in prayer has been a priceless gift, and I thank God for your faithfulness.

Finally, I offer my deepest gratitude to the Father, the Son, and the Holy Spirit, whose boundless grace has guided and empowered me to write these words. God alone equips us to inspire, encourage,

and serve others, and His promise in Isaiah 55:11 reminds me, *"So is my word that goes out from my mouth: It will not return to me empty, but will accomplish what I desire and achieve the purpose for which I sent it."* This work is a reflection of His purpose, not mine, and I pray it will glorify Him in every way.

A Word About the Stories in This Book

The testimonies and stories shared throughout this book are sacred. Many reflect people whose lives have deeply impacted my own journey with Christ. Some I've known personally, and others whose faith inspired me from afar.

To honor privacy, some names and identifying details have been changed. A few narratives have been thoughtfully combined or adapted to highlight the spiritual insights God impressed upon my heart to share. Every effort has been made to preserve the integrity, spirit, and truth of each testimony with care, compassion, and deep reverence.

Foreword

Faith That Transforms: God's Power and Authority Unlocked is more than just a book. It's a life-changing journey. Through Scripture, personal testimonies, and powerful real-world applications, Anthony Vaughn unpacks the true essence of faith and how it can radically transform your life. This book doesn't just inspire belief; it empowers you to walk boldly in the divine authority God has already given you.

Each chapter peels back the layers of faith, revealing how it deepens our relationship with God, fuels our purpose, and unlocks the supernatural power and authority available to us as believers. With clarity and wisdom, Anthony Vaughn masterfully explains why faith is not just important, it's essential for living a victorious and fulfilling life.

Whether you are seeking deeper spiritual growth, longing to experience God's power in action, or simply desiring to strengthen your trust in Him, Faith That Transforms will guide you every step of the way. It challenges you to rise above fear and doubt, embrace God's promises, and step into a life of unwavering faith and supernatural breakthrough.

It is my absolute honor to recommend Faith That Transforms: God's Power and Authority Unlocked to anyone ready to embrace a deeper, unshakable faith and experience the fullness of God's promises. Prepare to be challenged, inspired, and transformed!

Pastor Emeritus Bishop Walter S. Thomas, Sr.

New Psalmist Baptist Church

Presiding Prelate of The Kingdom Association of Covenant Pastors

Contents

Preface _____ 9

Introduction: The Greater Faith — Entering the Heart of God _ 11

1. The Foundation of Faith _____ 15
   Renewal of the Mind _____ 19

2. Walking in the Power of God's Word _____ 29
   Turning Pain into Purpose _____ 35

3. Faith That Moves Mountains _____ 41
   Returning What Doesn't Fit_____ 49

4. The Transformative Power of Trust _____ 54
   Walking on Holy Ground _____ 59

5. Faith as the Divine Connector_____ 69
   Faith is the Gift of Grace_____ 75

6. Living Out Your Beliefs Daily _____ 80
   "The God Who Laughs" _____ 87

7. Praying with Power and Confidence _____ 91
   The Thrill of Victory, The Agony of Faith_____ 97

8. Overcoming Obstacles to Faith _____ 102
   Faith on the Fast Track _____ 111

9. Accessing Divine Power Through Faith _____ 117
   Faith in the Storm_____ 120

10. Faith That Heals _____ 125
    Overcoming Doubt and Trusting God's Direction_____ 129

11. Operating in the Dominion Given to You _____ 138
    Choosing the Voice of Faith_____ 142

12. The Trials of Faith _____ 154
    Permission Granted _____ 158
    When Hope Calls, Faith Answers _____ 164

13. The Role of Obedience _____ 170
    Faith: The Master Key to the Supernatural_____ 174

14. Faith for the Impossible _____ 183
    The Power of a Profession of Faith _____ 186

15. Living as an Overcomer in Every Season _____ 194
    Walking in God's Power and Authority by Faith ____ 198

About the Author _____ **205**

Preface

In a world of shifting values and uncertain foundations, what sustains the soul?

Faith.

Not the kind we wear like a badge, but the kind that transforms. The kind that anchors, empowers, and awakens us to the reality of God's presence and power.

This book was birthed in prayer and deep communion with God. It is not just a collection of spiritual thoughts; it is an invitation to step into a deeper relationship with Him, where faith is not merely something we profess, but something that reshapes us.

Faith is not passive. It doesn't just help us survive life's storms, it compels us to walk on water. It seeks truth in Christ Jesus, yearns for God's presence, and unlocks His supernatural power and authority in our lives. In a time when surface-level belief is no longer enough, God is calling us higher into a faith that transforms both life's circumstances and the inner condition of our hearts.

To understand this kind of faith, we must look to the One who embodied it perfectly: Jesus Christ. His life, death, and resurrection are the ultimate demonstration of trust in the Father and power over sin, death, and darkness. Jesus didn't come merely to teach or inspire. He came to reconcile us to God and to model what it means to live fully surrendered in faith.

"The Word became flesh and dwelt among us." —John 1:14

Jesus stepped into our brokenness not as a distant deity, but as One who shared in our human experience. He understands our pain, but

He doesn't stop there He transforms it. In Christ, the divine meets the human. And through Him, we are invited to reflect God's glory in how we live, love, and serve.

This kind of faith asks something of us. It is more than belief it is surrender.

It's entrusting our hearts, our futures, and even our fears to the God who already gave everything for us. If Jesus entrusted Himself to humanity, how much more should we entrust ourselves to Him?

"Apart from Me you can do nothing." —*John 15:5*

Faith that transforms is not static. It is a living force that compels action, molds character, and aligns us with divine purpose. It causes us to live in such a way that the world no longer simply hears about Jesus but sees Him in us.

The faith Jesus lived and now calls us to embrace is not just a belief system.

It is a way of life.

It is the power of God made manifest in the lives of His people.

Through this faith, we are not only saved but also empowered to bring healing to the broken places around us. When our lives are transformed, they become invitations for others to enter the redemptive story written by the hand of a loving and faithful God.

As you journey through the pages of this book, my prayer is this:

You won't just learn about faith.

You'll experience it.

You'll embrace the kind of faith that unlocks God's power and authority for everlasting change in your life, in your calling, and in your communion with Him.

-Anthony Vaughn

Introduction:
The Greater Faith —
Entering the Heart of God

Have you ever considered that faith touches every part of your life? Whether acknowledged or not, it shapes your thoughts, guides your choices, and influences your actions. Faith is not merely a religious idea, it's a divine thread woven into the fabric of everyday life. From trusting the sun will rise to believing in the unseen power of God, faith quietly sustains us. Spiritually, it is the foundation by which we align with God's purpose, receive His promises, and walk in His authority.

But then comes the deeper question:

What does God desire from the greater faith He calls me to?

This is not the cry of a soul seeking mere blessings. It is the awakening of a heart yearning for the fullness of God's being, for the glory of His presence and the weight of His voice. Greater faith isn't about trying harder to believe it's about being transformed to see clearer. It is stepping past comfort and into the radiance of God's heart and power.

> *"But without faith it is impossible to please Him, for he who comes to God must believe that He is, and that He is a rewarder of those who diligently seek Him."*
> *(Hebrews 11:6)*

Faith is more than the beginning of our walk with God. It is the bridge into His mystery. When it grows, when it's tested and refined it not only reveals what God can do, it reveals who He is.

To behold Him is to be changed by Him.

As Paul wrote,

> *"But we all, with unveiled face, beholding as in a mirror the glory of the Lord, are being transformed into the same image from glory to glory..."*
> (2 Corinthians 3:18)

This kind of faith lifts the veil. It brings you into a place where God's character is no longer distant, His purpose no longer abstract, and His presence no longer occasional. Faith becomes more than belief it becomes communion. The kind Moses had when he spoke to God "face to face, as a man speaks to his friend" (Exodus 33:11).

In this sacred transformation, your mind shifts. The patterns of this world loosen their grip, and your life begins to change. That's the fruit of greater faith: not just revelation, but obedience. Not just inspiration, but surrender.

So, what does God want from your greater faith?

He wants you.

Not just your belief in what He can do, but your full participation in who He is. He wants you to draw near, to enter the deep waters of His sovereignty, and to be remade in the image of His Son.

> *"Deep calls to deep at the noise of Your waterfalls;*
> *All Your waves and billows have gone over me."*
> (Psalm 42:7)

Greater faith is the call to dive into those depths. To live from them.

And in those waters.

You will see.

You will know.

You will live.

This is your invitation.

Let faith transform you. Let it unlock the power and authority God placed within you for a life that reflects His glory.

Now, turn the page. The journey begins here.

"Unshakable belief is not built in comfort. It's forged in surrender, brick by brick, on the foundation of God's unchanging truth."

"Therefore everyone who hears these words of mine and puts them into practice is like a wise man who built his house on the rock."
— *Matthew 7:24 (NIV)*

Chapter 1:
THE FOUNDATION OF FAITH

Faith That Anchors: Building a Life That Cannot Be Shaken

There comes a point in every soul's journey when surface answers no longer suffice. When the storms of life press in, when our strength falters, and when all the things we once leaned on begin to crumble. What remains?

The answer, echoing through centuries of hardship and hope, is faith.

Not faith as a vague sentiment or inherited ritual, but living, breathing faith. A divine tether that binds us to the heart of God.

This is not faith for convenience. It's the kind of faith that steadies trembling hands and quiets anxious thoughts. Faith that doesn't merely survive the storm but learns to move with the wind, trusting the One who commands both the tempest and the calm.

This is the faith that transforms.

This is the faith that anchors.

A Clearer Kind of Faith

Faith isn't wishful thinking. It isn't emotional hype or blind optimism. Hebrews 11:1 defines it plainly:

> *"Now faith is the assurance of things hoped for, the conviction of things not seen."*

Faith is divine assurance, rooted not in how we feel, but in who God is. It is spiritual clarity in a fog-covered world. It's how we see the unseen, how we walk when the path ahead disappears.

Picture a seasoned sailor adrift in open waters. The stars are hidden. The shoreline is lost. But he has his compass. He has trust.

That's faith, not the absence of the storm, but confidence in the One who leads us through it.

Consider the disciples in Mark 4, terrified in a boat as waves threatened to consume them. Jesus was there, not absent, not indifferent, but asleep in perfect peace. And when they called on Him, He calmed the storm with a word. That same Jesus anchors us now.

Faith That Changes Everything

Faith doesn't always change our circumstances. But it always changes us.

It lifts our eyes off what is temporary and uncertain, and locks them onto the eternal, unshakable character of God. When we walk by faith, we're no longer confined to what seems possible, we step into alignment with a God for whom nothing is impossible.

How many storms have you faced, unsure of what tomorrow held, yet somehow carried by a peace you couldn't explain? That was faith whispering: God is here. Keep going.

When we live anchored in that kind of faith, the winds may still howl, but we are not moved. We are held.

Where Is Your Anchor?

Storms will come. Winds will rise. But those anchored in Christ will not be shaken.

So pause for a moment.

Where is your anchor today?

Why Faith Is Essential

> *"Without faith it is impossible to please God."* — Hebrews 11:6

Faith isn't optional, it's vital. It's not a spiritual add-on, but our life-line. Through faith, we lay hold of God's promises, step into His presence, and find strength to endure the unseen.

Without it, we drift.

With it, we're anchored, not to outcomes or comfort, but to the eternal, unshakable character of God.

1. Faith Anchors Us to God

When fear howls and uncertainty rises, faith holds us steady. It doesn't remove the chaos, but it roots us in the One who never changes. Like an anchor in deep waters, faith keeps us grounded while God writes His story in us, even when the ending isn't yet clear.

2. Faith Opens the Door to Intimacy

Faith isn't just believing in what God can do, it's trusting in who He is. Hebrews 11:6 continues:

> *"He rewards those who earnestly seek Him."*

Faith pulls us into God's presence. It says, "I'm not just here for answers, I'm here for You." This is where religion fades and relationship begins. Where we move from performance into presence.

3. Faith Is a Daily Journey

Faith is more than a moment, it's a movement. A lifestyle of trust. It's how we live, how we relate, and how we pray.

> ➢ Faith Builds Relationship
> Like Abraham, we follow even when the path is unclear, because we trust the One leading us.

➢ Faith Requires Vulnerability
Psalm 62:8 urges:
"Pour out your hearts to Him..."
Real faith brings the questions, the disappointments, the mess, and lays them at Jesus' feet, trusting that He meets us there.

➢ Faith Fuels Communion
Faith transforms prayer from crisis management into holy conversation. We stop begging and start partnering.
Hebrews 4:16 invites us to approach God's throne boldly, not with performance, but with trust.

4. Faith Builds What Stands

Jesus told of two builders, one on sand, the other on rock. Both faced storms, but only one house stood. Why? The foundation.

> *"Everyone who hears these words of mine and puts them into practice is like a wise man who built his house on the rock."*
> — *Matthew 7:24*

Our foundation is the Word of God.

Faith grows not in noise, but in quiet, daily trust, fed by Scripture, shaped by presence, and strengthened by obedience.

A Life That Cannot Be Shaken

Let faith anchor you.

Let it shape how you live, how you love, and how you see.

You weren't made for fear. You were made to stand. To shine. To endure.

The journey won't always be easy, but it will always be worth it.

Because when your life is built on real, raw, relentless faith, nothing can shake you.

Closing Prayer

Dear God, thank You for the gift of faith. Teach us to trust You more deeply and build our lives on the solid foundation of Your Word. Help us walk in obedience and draw closer to You in every season. May our faith be a light to others and a testimony of Your transformative power. In Jesus' name, Amen.

~❖~

Renewal of the Mind

> *"Do not conform to the pattern of this world, but be transformed by the renewing of your mind. Then you will be able to test and approve what God's will is—His good, pleasing, and perfect will."*
> *– Romans 12:2*

Faith isn't just an idea; it's the power that rewires your thinking, transforms your perspective, and unlocks the supernatural authority of God. Faith is the bridge between the seen and unseen, the tangible and the eternal. It's not passive or static; it's alive, active, and shaping every decision we make. Without faith, it is impossible to please God (Hebrews 11:6). With faith, mountains move, storms calm, and lives are transformed.

The renewal of the mind begins with faith. A faith that trusts God's promises over the world's patterns. When Paul urged believers in Romans 12:2 not to conform to the world, he was calling them to break free from the limitations of human understanding and step into God's boundless possibilities. Faith rewires us to see life through God's eyes, allowing us to rise above fear, doubt, and the constraints of our circumstances.

Like the friends of the paralyzed man in Mark 2:5, faith isn't passive; it takes action. Their trust in Jesus led them to tear through a roof to bring their friend to healing. Faith moves, acts, and pursues, even when the odds seem insurmountable. And like Peter stepping out of

the boat, faith dares to walk on water, even in the midst of the storm (Matthew 14:29-31).

But faith also requires focus. Just as Peter sank when he shifted his gaze to the waves, we, too, falter when we focus on life's chaos instead of God's promises. Faith renews our mind by aligning it with heaven's perspective, enabling us to walk in boldness and peace, even in the face of uncertainty.

Faith doesn't merely sustain us. It transforms us. As we trust God more, we are transformed into His likeness, aligning our minds and hearts with His divine will.

> This is the power of faith: it makes us new, changes the way we think, and equips us to live out God's purpose with confidence and authority.

Renewal of the Mind: Living from the Inside Out

> *"Do not conform to the pattern of this world, but be transformed by the renewing of your mind. Then you will be able to test and approve what God's will is—His good, pleasing, and perfect will."*
> — *Romans 12:2*

What if the greatest battles you're fighting aren't around you, but within you? What if your future, your peace, your purpose, and your power, doesn't begin with your circumstances, but with the way you think?

Transformation begins not with behavior, but with belief. Not with effort, but with encounter. Not with striving, but with surrender. This is the invitation of Romans 12:2. Not simply to avoid worldly patterns, but to become something altogether new. To allow the Spirit of God to rewire your thoughts, reshape your desires, and realign your life with heaven's heartbeat.

Faith Is the Catalyst

Faith isn't a concept we carry in our minds. It's a fire that consumes and renews. It's the power that shatters strongholds, dismantles lies, and forges new pathways of hope, joy, and clarity in the soul.

> *"Without faith it is impossible to please God..."*
> — Hebrews 11:6

But hear this clearly:

> Faith is not passive. It doesn't wait for life to become easy. Faith activates. It pursues.

It presses forward even when nothing makes sense. Faith is the engine of renewal. The supernatural lens through which we begin to see not just what is, but what God says will be.

Through faith, your mind becomes a battleground where heaven claims victory.

Break the Mold of This World

Paul's command to "not conform" is a bold and urgent call. He's not asking you to tidy up your life or clean up your language. He's calling you to walk away from a system designed to keep you spiritually asleep.

> Too many believers are stuck on what I call the "treadmill life."

You're walking, moving, striving, but getting nowhere in Christ. You're active but not advancing. Busy but not breaking through. Faithless movement is not the same as forward motion in the Spirit.

The world teaches you to be ruled by fear, scarcity, pride, and performance. But faith teaches you to be led by love, abundance, humility, and grace. Let me be honest with you: the renewal of the mind isn't self-improvement; it's supernatural transformation by the pow-

er and glory of God Himself. It's letting God tear down the strongholds of deception and build monuments of truth in their place.

Think of it like this: The mind shaped by the world says, "I am what I do." But the mind renewed by faith says, "I am who God declares me to be." I am holy. I am set apart. I am anointed by God's grace.

Faith Acts. Faith Moves. Faith Risks.

The story of the paralyzed man in Mark 2 is more than a miracle of healing. It's a portrait of desperate, determined, and daring faith. His friends didn't wait for the perfect conditions. They climbed a roof. They tore it open. They acted on what they believed: If we can just get to Jesus, everything will change.

This is the kind of faith that renews the mind. It doesn't ask for permission. It doesn't wait for proof. It sees obstacles not as walls, but as doors waiting for God to open.

When was the last time your faith moved you to do something radical? When did it last shake you out of routine and pull you into risk?

Eyes on Jesus: The Focus of Renewed Faith

You know the story. When Peter stepped out of the boat in Matthew 14, his eyes were locked on Jesus, like a missile fixed on its target. He did the impossible: he walked on water. But the moment he shifted his focus from the Savior to the storm; he began to sink.

This is the daily battle for your mind.

> Distraction is the enemy of transformation.

If the enemy can't destroy you, he'll distract you, pulling your focus from God's promises to life's problems.

But a renewed mind refuses to be ruled by the waves. It anchors itself in truth. It lifts its eyes. It chooses, again and again, to fix its gaze on Jesus.

> *"You will keep in perfect peace those whose minds are steadfast,*
> *because they trust in you."*
> — Isaiah 26:3

Faith That Transforms

Let's break it down: Faith isn't just what we believe, it's how we become.

It's not about behavior modification. It's about being conformed to the image of Christ from the inside out (Romans 8:29).

As faith renews your mind, you begin to think with heaven's logic. You respond with Christ's compassion. You live not from lack, but from abundance, not from fear, but from love. Your thoughts stop echoing the lies of the enemy and start reflecting the heart of the Father.

"You begin to see what God sees. Feel what God feels. Desire what God desires. You don't just change, you become. This transformation is not merely a change in behavior; it represents a fundamental reformation of the heart. Your will begins to align with His. Your steps echo His purpose. His presence doesn't just visit, it dwells. That is the power of true transformation!"

How to Live a Renewed Life

This journey of transformation is not instant, but it is intentional. Here's how you can live it out daily:

1. Immerse Yourself in God's Word

Truth must be louder than lies. Let Scripture wash over you until God's thoughts become your thoughts.

> *"Sanctify them by the truth; your word is truth."* — John 17:17

2. Pray with Expectation

Prayer is where renewal breathes. Don't just talk—listen. Let the Holy Spirit reframe your worries with wisdom and ignite your fear with fire.

3. Practice Spiritual Discernment

A renewed mind doesn't believe everything it hears. It tests every thought, every motive, every influence against the voice of God.

> *"...Then you will be able to test and approve what God's will is..."*
> *— Romans 12:2*

4. Live in Godly Community

Renewal thrives in the presence of others running the same race. Surround yourself with voices that sharpen, stretch, and strengthen your faith.

5. Obey Promptly

Transformation doesn't wait for perfect conditions; it moves in step with the Spirit. As your mind is renewed, your actions will follow. Do what God says, when He says it.

Renewal of the Mind

> *"Do not conform to the pattern of this world, but be transformed by the renewing of your mind. Then you will be able to test and approve what God's will is—His good, pleasing, and perfect will."*
> *– Romans 12:2*

Faith is more than acknowledging God's existence; it is trusting Him fully, even when the path ahead is unclear. It is the confidence that He is faithful to His promises and the assurance that He rewards those who earnestly seek Him (Hebrews 11:6). Faith is the founda-

tion of a transformed mind, a renewed spirit, and a life aligned with God's will.

Faith: The Portal to Heaven's Power

Faith is not merely belief; it is the divine portal through which we access the reality of God's Kingdom. It opens the way for us to step into the fullness of His presence, power, and grace. Faith invites Heaven into Earth's circumstances, positioning us to experience God's supernatural work in the midst of our daily lives.

Romans 12:2 urges us to be transformed by the renewing of our minds. That renewal begins with faith, a radical trust that aligns our thinking with God's truth rather than human limitation. Faith isn't passive; it is the active embrace of God's promises, enabling us to live beyond what we see or feel. As Malachi 3:10 declares, "I will open the windows of heaven and pour you out a blessing, that there shall not be room enough to receive it." These blessings are not limited to material provision; they include peace in uncertainty, strength in weakness, and joy in suffering, evidence of God's presence at work within us.

Faith: A Bridge to the Unseen

Faith is the supernatural bridge between our human frailty and God's divine ability. It reaches beyond circumstances and connects us to the eternal. Hebrews 11:6 reminds us, "Without faith, it is impossible to please God, because anyone who comes to Him must believe that He exists and that He rewards those who earnestly seek Him."

Faith shifts our vision, from what is visible to what God has already established in the unseen. When we trust Him fully and live in obedience to His Word, faith becomes the conduit through which His wisdom, provision, and guidance flow. It empowers us to act not just in hope, but in confident expectation.

Application: Living by Faith Today

Faith is not only for moments of crisis or spiritual highs, it's a daily choice to believe God, walk with Him, and expect His presence in every area of life. So ask yourself:

Where is God calling you to trust Him more deeply?

Is it in your finances, your relationships, your calling, or your waiting?

Step through the portal. Trust Him not just for what He can do, but for who He is. When you do, you won't just receive from Heaven, you'll live from it.

The Portals of Heaven in Action

➢ Faith doesn't only provide access to material blessings; it transforms us by granting access to God's very presence. This is where transformation occurs, where fear is replaced by confidence, and weakness is replaced by strength.

The Bible provides numerous examples of faith opening Heaven's portals:

➢ The Centurion's Faith: In Matthew 8:5-13, the Roman centurion's trust in Jesus' authority brought miraculous healing for his servant. Jesus marveled at his faith, saying, *"I have not found anyone in Israel with such great faith."*

➢ The Woman with the Issue of Blood: In Mark 5:25-34, her faith led her to touch Jesus' garment, and she was instantly healed. Her faith opened the gateway to God's power.

➢ The Friends of the Paralyzed Man: In Mark 2:5, the bold faith of these friends led them to break through a roof to bring their friend to Jesus. Their faith unlocked both healing and forgiveness.

Each of these examples demonstrates that faith acts as a divine activator, unlocking Heaven's power and enabling miracles.

Faith in Action

Faith is not passive; it demands action. It requires us to step out in obedience, even when the path is uncertain. Consider Peter walking on water in Matthew 14:29-31. His faith opened the gateway to a miraculous moment with Jesus, but when he focused on the storm rather than Jesus, doubt crept in, and he began to sink.

This teaches us that faith requires bold steps and a steadfast focus on Christ. When our eyes remain on Him, the portals of Heaven stay open, allowing His presence to sustain and empower us.

In closing, Faith is not just about believing; it is about trusting God enough to act. It is the key to unlocking God's unlimited power. When you allow faith to transform your mind, it renews your heart, aligns your steps, and brings you into the fullness of God's promises. Trust Him completely, for He is able to do *exceedingly abundantly above all we ask or think*" (Ephesians 3:20). Let your faith rise today, and experience the transformative power of God.

Prayer:

Heavenly Father,

Thank You for the gift of faith that renews our minds and transforms our lives. We ask for Your guidance as we step into deeper trust and alignment with Your will. Renew our hearts and minds through Your Word and help us to reject the distractions of this world.

Lord, we declare that Your promises are true, and we trust You to open the portals of Heaven over our lives. Let Your power, presence, and grace flow freely as we walk in faith. Strengthen our resolve to step out in obedience and trust You in every season.

Father God, we surrender our fears and doubts to You. Even now, fill us with unwavering confidence in Your plan, and let our faith be a beacon that inspires others to seek and trust You. Transform us from the inside out, that we may glorify You in all we do.

We pray this in the name of Jesus Christ, the author and perfecter of our faith. May Your will be done, and may Your blessings overflow in our lives.

Amen

Chapter 2:

WALKING IN THE POWER OF GOD'S WORD

Let's explore the synergy between faith and authority, demonstrating how believers can walk boldly in God's power, overcome obstacles, and fulfill His purposes. Faith is not just a personal belief, it's an active force that unlocks divine authority and manifests heaven's power on earth.

Faith That Transforms: Walking in Divine Authority

> Faith does more than change your heart; it transforms your worldview and interactions with the world.

When you fully grasp the authority God has entrusted to you, your faith becomes more than a personal belief system.

Imagine being deputized by God to carry out His will on earth. Why would the Creator of the universe empower imperfect people with such immense responsibility? The answer lies in His love and purpose. God invites us to not only believe in Him but also to partner with Him, using faith to enact His will and demonstrate His power in a broken world.

Faith as Authority: A Divine Delegation

Being deputized means being granted authority to act on someone else's behalf. In the same way, when God gives us faith, He isn't just

asking for trust, He's commissioning us to carry His authority into every situation we face. This authority is not earned; it is a gift of grace granted through our relationship with Christ.

In Matthew 28:18-20, Jesus declares, "All authority in heaven and on earth has been given to me. Therefore go and make disciples of all nations..." In this passage, Jesus transfers His authority to His followers, empowering them to continue His mission. Similarly, Luke 10:19 tells us, "I have given you authority to trample on snakes and scorpions and to overcome all the power of the enemy; nothing will harm you."

This authority is not a tool for personal gain but a sacred responsibility to align with God's will and bring His kingdom to the brokenness of the world. Faith is the mechanism through which we access this authority, and with it comes a profound responsibility to steward it wisely.

> Faith becomes a channel for God's power when it aligns our will, thoughts, and actions with His purposes.

This alignment creates a spiritual conduit through which God's authority and presence can manifest in our lives and the world. Here's a deeper look at how this transformation happens:

1. Faith Aligns Us with God's Will

When we trust God completely, our desires, priorities, and decisions begin to reflect His will. This alignment is crucial because God's power flows most freely when we act in accordance with His purposes. For example, in the Bible, Jesus often emphasized faith as the key to miracles, faith that God's plans will prevail, even when circumstances seem impossible (Mark 11:22-24).

2. Faith Activates Spiritual Authority

Through faith, we recognize the authority God has given us as His children. Jesus promised that those who believe in Him would do

"greater works" (John 14:12). This authority isn't about personal power; it's about being vessels through which God's will is carried out. When we exercise this faith, whether through prayer, speaking truth, or acting in obedience, we allow God to work through us to bring healing, transformation, and hope.

3. Faith Overcomes Fear and Doubt

Doubt and fear can block the flow of God's power because they limit our ability to trust Him fully. When we walk in faith, we overcome these barriers, creating a pathway for God's influence to be felt in our lives and the lives of others. For example, Peter walked on water when he kept his focus on Jesus, but he began to sink when fear distracted him (Matthew 14:29-30). Faith keeps us steady and open to the supernatural.

4. Faith Fuels Bold Actions

Faith compels us to act boldly, even when we don't see the outcome. This courage often inspires others and creates ripple effects. For instance, Moses' faith led him to part the Red Sea, enabling the Israelites to escape Pharaoh's army (Exodus 14:21-22). His obedience was not just a personal act of faith but a demonstration of God's power to an entire nation.

5. Faith Produces Spiritual Fruit

When we live by faith, we bear the fruits of the Spirit—love, joy, peace, patience, kindness, and more (Galatians 5:22-23). These fruits impact our interactions, relationships, and communities, drawing others to experience God's transformative power. A life rooted in faith becomes a testimony to God's goodness and an invitation for others to trust Him.

6. Faith Amplifies Prayer

Faith, infused prayer has the power to change circumstances. James 5:16 says, "The prayer of a righteous person is powerful and effec-

tive." When we pray with faith, believing that God hears and responds, we invite His intervention in ways that can heal, restore, and uplift.

7. Faith Illuminates Hope

Faith isn't just about the present; it also gives us hope for the future. This hope can transform how we face challenges, inspiring perseverance and resilience. When others see this hope in us, it can lead them to seek the source of our strength, ultimately pointing them to God.

In summary, faith is not a passive belief but an active partnership with God. It opens the door for His power to flow through our words, actions, and prayers, bringing transformation to us and the world around us. By trusting in His promises and stepping out in obedience, we become instruments of His divine purposes, capable of making a profound impact.

A Force to Be Reckoned With

Faith is not passive; it is an active, dynamic force that transforms everything it touches.

> It is the catalyst for miracles, healing, deliverance, and transformation.

Take the story of Peter walking on water in Matthew 14:29-31. At Jesus' command, Peter stepped out of the boat and walked on the waves. For a brief moment, his faith enabled him to defy natural laws. But when he shifted his focus to the storm, doubt crept in, and he began to sink.

This story illustrates an important principle: faith isn't just about believing in God's power, it's about trusting His authority even when circumstances seem overwhelming. Faith connects us to God's limitless power, making it a force that truly changes lives.

Why Would God Entrust Us with Such Power?

God grants us authority out of His desire for relationship and partnership. Humanity was created in His image, with the capacity to reflect His character and carry out His will. Through faith, God invites us to be co-laborers in His redemptive work on earth.

God doesn't delegate authority because of our strength or worthiness. He does so because of His grace, using ordinary people to accomplish extraordinary things. This empowerment underscores His love and His purpose for our lives.

How Faith Transforms Us and the World

Faith transforms not only our lives but also the lives of those around us. It reshapes how we see ourselves, empowering us to become ambassadors of Christ. Instead of succumbing to fear or doubt, faith enables us to see challenges as opportunities for God's power to be revealed.

Faith also transforms the world by inviting God's presence into every situation. When we pray in faith, we align with His will, and His power flows into the natural realm. Faith becomes the bridge between heaven and earth, bringing divine solutions to human problems.

Practical Ways to Walk in Authority Through Faith

1. Know the Source of Your Authority

Your authority comes from Christ, not from your own strength or merit. Stay rooted in His Word, and understand the promises He has given.

2. Speak with Boldness

Declare God's promises over your life and circumstances. His Word does not return void (Isaiah 55:11).

3. Act in Obedience

Faith without action is dead (James 2:26). Step out in obedience, trusting that God will provide what you need.

4. Pray with Expectation

Prayer is where faith and authority converge. Pray boldly and expectantly, but remain surrendered to His will.

5. Remain Humble

Remember, your authority is a gift of grace. Use it to serve others and glorify God, not to elevate yourself. Faith that transforms is a faith that acts. It recognizes the authority God has entrusted to us and uses it to fulfill His will on earth. Such faith requires surrender, boldness, and a deep trust in God's power and plan.

Understanding Authority: Jesus' Delegation of Power to Believers

Authority is the right to act on behalf of someone greater. As believers, we walk in the authority of Jesus Christ. Luke 10:19 states, "Behold, I give you the authority to trample on serpents and scorpions, and over all the power of the enemy, and nothing shall by any means hurt you."

This authority wasn't just for Jesus' disciples; it extends to every believer. It is not something we strive to earn; it's a gift to be received and used confidently. Just as a police officer's badge represents their delegated authority, believers act under the authority of heaven, backed by the power of God.

The Connection Between Faith and Authority

Faith activates authority. Without faith, authority remains dormant. Matthew 8:5-13 recounts the story of a centurion who understood this principle. He told Jesus, "Just say the word, and my servant will

be healed." Jesus marveled at his faith because the centurion believed in the power of His Word to bring healing.

Faith acknowledges God's authority and responds in obedience. When we trust His Word and act on it, His power is released.

Authority through faith isn't for a select few; it is the birthright of every believer. As you walk in God's power, speak His promises, and face challenges with faith, you'll witness transformation not only in your life but in the world around you. Faith is a force that bridges heaven and earth, one that God has entrusted to you.

Prayer:

Lord, thank You for the gift of faith and the authority You have entrusted to us. Teach us to walk boldly in that authority, aligning our actions with Your will. Help us trust in Your power even when the path is unclear. May our faith transform not only our lives but the world around us, bringing glory to Your name. Amen.

In a world desperate for healing, one woman's life would change the course of history forever. From her pain came power. From her cells came salvation for millions. Witness the true story of Henrietta Lacks, a tale of faith that refuses to die and a legacy that lives on.

Turning Pain into Purpose

> *"And we know that in all things God works for the good of those who love Him, who have been called according to His purpose."*
> — *Romans 8:28*

The story of Henrietta Lacks is one of profound faith, resilience, and an eternal purpose birthed out of pain. Though her earthly life was brief, her legacy became an everlasting testament to God's divine plan. Like the life, death, and resurrection of Jesus Christ, her suffering bore fruit that transformed humanity. Henrietta's cells, known as

HeLa cells, became an unstoppable force for healing, just as the sacrifice of Christ brought redemption to the world. Her story reminds us that, even in suffering, God's purpose prevails.

A Life Interrupted, A Legacy Eternal

Born in 1920 in rural Virginia, Henrietta Lacks was a young, vibrant African American woman filled with hope despite the hardships of her time. As a mother of five, her days were marked by toil, love, and faith. In 1951, at the age of 31, Henrietta was diagnosed with cervical cancer, a diagnosis that carried unimaginable pain. Yet, her life, like the grain of wheat Jesus spoke of in John 12:24, was destined to fall to the ground and bear much fruit.

Henrietta's treatment at Johns Hopkins Hospital was a turning point. According to news accounts, without her knowledge or consent, a sample of her tumor cells was taken. Scientists discovered that these cells, unlike others, did not die in the lab. They reproduced endlessly, becoming the first "immortalized" human cell line. These cells, called HeLa, after Henrietta Lacks, became the cornerstone of countless medical breakthroughs, from the polio vaccine to cancer treatments and in-vitro fertilization. Her cells played a vital role in the COVID-19 pandemic.

Though Henrietta passed away, her cells carried on a purpose that would save and improve millions of lives. It is a profound reminder that, in God's hands, our pain can be transformed into a legacy of hope.

Faith That Refuses to Die

Henrietta's story echoes the life of Jesus Christ, whose suffering brought eternal salvation. Like Henrietta, Jesus faced immense pain and injustice. He, too, was misunderstood, and His purpose was not fully realized by those around Him until after His death. Yet, through faith, Jesus demonstrated the power of God to redeem even the darkest situations.

Faith is a force that refuses to die. It finds a way to break through barriers and fulfill its God-given purpose. Henrietta's cells symbolize this truth, they were meant to perish, yet they multiplied. Similarly, faith allows us to transcend the limits of our circumstances and participate in God's eternal plan.

> *"For I know the plans I have for you,"* declares the Lord, *"plans to prosper you and not to harm you, plans to give you hope and a future." — Jeremiah 29:11*

Henrietta's life reminds us that our earthly experience is temporary, but the impact of our faith and purpose is eternal.

Jesus, Lazarus, and Eternal Impact

Henrietta's story is reminiscent of another: the resurrection of Lazarus in John 11. Lazarus was a dear friend of Jesus, and his death brought deep sorrow. Yet, Jesus declared, "This sickness will not end in death. No, it is for God's glory so that God's Son may be glorified through it" (John 11:4). Lazarus's resurrection became a testament to God's power and a foreshadowing of Jesus' own victory over death.

Similarly, Henrietta's cells, though taken without her consent, became a symbol of hope and transformation. They serve as a reminder that God can use any situation, even those marked by injustice, for His glory.

Turning Pain into Purpose

To transform our pain into purpose, we must:

1. Acknowledge the Pain

Henrietta endured physical suffering, but her life was not defined by it. Like Jesus in the Garden of Gethsemane, we must bring our pain to God in faith.

> *"Come to me, all you who are weary and burdened, and I will give you rest."* — *Matthew 11:28*

2. Seek God's Perspective

Pain often blinds us to the bigger picture, but faith helps us see God's hand at work. Henrietta's family initially struggled with the injustice of her cells being used without consent, but they later embraced her legacy as a gift to the world.

3. Use Your Pain for Good

Just as Henrietta's cells became a force for healing, we can channel our pain into purpose. Whether it's advocating for justice, creating solutions, or offering support to others, our pain can become a testimony.

> *"What you intended to harm me, God intended it for good to accomplish what is now being done, the saving of many lives."* — *Genesis 50:20*

4. Trust God's Timing

Henrietta's family didn't learn of her impact until decades later. Like Lazarus's resurrection, God's purpose unfolds in His perfect time.

Embrace Your Eternal Purpose

Henrietta's story challenges us to view our lives through the lens of eternity. What pain are you carrying? How might God use it to bless others? Surrender your struggles to Him and trust that He will bring beauty from ashes.

Prayer: Transforming Pain into Purpose

Heavenly Father,

We thank You for the life of Henrietta Lacks, a testament to Your ability to turn pain into purpose. Help us to trust in Your divine plan, even when we cannot see the outcome. Teach us to surrender our struggles to You, knowing that You work all things for good. Strengthen our faith, Lord, so we may walk boldly in the purpose You have set before us. Transform our lives into a living testimony of Your grace, love, and power.

In Jesus' name, Amen.

Henrietta Lacks's legacy reminds us that our human experience is temporary, but the impact of a life lived in faith is eternal. Through Christ, our pain can become purpose, and our suffering can bring about healing, not just for us, but for generations to come. Trust God with your story, and watch how He uses it to bring hope to the world.

"Mountains don't move at the sound of fear; they move when faith speaks with the authority of heaven."

"If you have faith as a mustard seed... it will move; and nothing will be impossible for you."
— Matthew 17:20 (NKJV)

Chapter 3:

FAITH THAT MOVES MOUNTAINS

Faith That Moves Mountains: A Transformative Journey

The disciples gathered around Jesus, their faces clouded with confusion and disappointment. Moments earlier, they had faced a daunting challenge, a demon-possessed boy brought to them by his desperate father. They had tried to cast out the demon, to free the boy from his suffering, but their efforts had failed. Now, standing before Jesus, they sought answers.

"Why couldn't we drive it out?" one of them asked, his voice tinged with frustration.

Jesus looked at them, His gaze both piercing and compassionate. "Because you have so little faith," He replied.

> "Truly I tell you, if you have faith as small as a mustard seed, you can say to this mountain, 'Move from here to there,' and it will move. Nothing will be impossible for you."

The Power of Faith to Transform

This exchange wasn't just about the disciples' inability to help the boy. It was a lesson about the nature of faith, a faith that transforms not only hearts but the very landscape of our lives. Jesus wasn't simply speaking in metaphors when He said that faith could move

mountains. He was pointing to the tangible, transformative power of belief when it is aligned with God's will.

> a faith that transforms not only hearts
> but the very landscape of our lives

When Jesus healed the boy, He didn't merely perform a miracle; He demonstrated the difference between faith and doubt, between trust and uncertainty. The "mountain" in this story wasn't a physical one, it was the obstacle of the demon tormenting the child, an obstacle the disciples couldn't overcome because their faith was incomplete.

Understanding Mountains and Mustard Seeds

The "mountain" is a metaphor for the insurmountable challenges in our lives, those moments when we feel overwhelmed, powerless, or defeated. It could be a chronic illness, a broken relationship, financial hardship, or spiritual struggles. We all face mountains that seem immovable.

Jesus' reference to a mustard seed, the smallest of seeds known in His time, was intentional. He wanted the disciples to understand that faith doesn't have to be massive to be effective. Even the tiniest bit of true faith, when placed in a mighty God, can achieve the impossible.

But what does it take to have this kind of faith? And how do we avoid turning faith into a wishful, unrealistic expectation that everything will happen the way we want?

Faith vs. Wishful Thinking

Faith that transforms isn't a spiritual strategy to get what we want. It's not about using belief as a lever to bend outcomes in our favor. True faith isn't projection, its surrender. It trusts God's power, submits to His timing, and aligns with His purpose, even when it collides with our desires.

There's a profound distinction between faith and wishful thinking, though they may look similar on the surface. Both carry hope. But only one is anchored in truth.

As my former pastor, Bishop Walter S. Thomas, Sr., once helped me understand:

Is wishful thinking the same as faith?

Wishful thinking is rooted in our preferences and limited perspective. It hopes for comfort, control, and ease, often without the cost of transformation. It looks for quick fixes, not deep formation.

Faith, by contrast, is grounded in humility and trust in God's sovereignty. It dares to say, "Even if the answer is no or wait, I still trust You." It moves beyond optimism. It endures. It requires action, obedience, and deep surrender.

Faith doesn't depend on favorable circumstances; it thrives in spite of them. It strengthens us when everything else shakes. It builds patience, peace, and resilience.

So how can we know if what we call "faith" is real, or just spiritualized wishing?

Ask:

Are we seeking God's will, or simply asking Him to fulfill ours?

Are we willing to be refined, or only looking to be rescued?

Authentic faith transforms not because it controls outcomes, but because it anchors us to the eternal, even while the storms of life rage around us.

Let's choose that kind of faith.

Not the illusion of control, but the peace of surrender.

Not a hollow hope, but a faith that holds.

How to Cultivate Transformative Faith

1. Consult God First

Before making any major decision, seek God's guidance through prayer. Ask Him to reveal His will and to align your heart with His plan.

2. Trust His Timing

Faith often involves waiting. Mountains don't move on our schedule but on God's. Trust that His timing is perfect, even when it seems delayed.

3. Take Action with Wisdom

Faith isn't passive. It requires steps of obedience, but those steps should be grounded in prayer, discernment, and responsibility.

4. Anchor Yourself in Scripture

God's Word is filled with examples of faith in action, Abraham leaving his homeland, David facing Goliath, and Esther risking her life to save her people. Learn from their stories and apply their lessons to your own life.

Your Mountains and God's Power

What are the mountains in your life? Are you facing a health crisis, a failing marriage, or a dream that feels out of reach? These challenges may seem insurmountable, but they are not too big for God. Faith as small as a mustard seed, when placed in Him, can move the largest obstacles.

Remember Joseph, who endured betrayal, slavery, and imprisonment before rising to power in Egypt. His faith didn't eliminate the challenges, but it transformed his perspective and allowed God to use those difficulties for good.

Transformative faith is not abstract; it is practical, powerful, and deeply personal. Whatever your mountain may be, place it in God's hands and trust Him to do the impossible.

Jesus' Promise: Analyzing Matthew 17:20

Jesus' words in Matthew 17:20 are both profound and challenging:

> *"If you have faith as small as a mustard seed, you can say to this mountain, 'Move from here to there,' and it will move. Nothing will be impossible for you."*

Here, Jesus highlights three truths about mountain-moving faith:

1. **Faith, no matter how small, has immense power:** The mustard seed, one of the tiniest seeds, holds the potential for incredible growth. Even the smallest measure of faith, when planted and nurtured, can produce miraculous results.

2. **Mountains represent impossible obstacles:** Jesus wasn't speaking of literal geological formations but of the towering problems in our lives, fear, sickness, lack, broken relationships.

3. **Faith requires action**: He instructed His followers to speak to the mountain. Faith isn't passive; it demands that we declare God's promises and take bold steps forward.

Jesus' promise wasn't about the size of our faith but the greatness of our God. A mustard seed of faith, rooted in His power, is enough to move the immovable.

The Power of Speaking in Faith: Declaring God's Will into Situations

Faith that moves mountains isn't silent, it speaks. Proverbs 18:21 reminds us, *"The tongue has the power of life and death."* What we say shapes our reality. When we align our words with God's promises,

we release His power into the world around us. When Jesus cursed the fig tree in Mark 11:12-14, His words carried authority. The next day, the tree was withered. In the same way, when we speak in faith, declaring healing, provision, or breakthrough, we activate the authority God has given us.

Practical ways to speak in faith:

1. **Declare God's Word: Speak Scriptures over your situation.** For example, if you need provision, declare Philippians 4:19, *"My God will supply all your needs according to His riches in glory."*

2. **Pray Boldly:** Instead of timid, uncertain prayers, approach God with confidence, trusting His promises.

3. **Command Obstacles:** Just as Jesus told the storm to be still, speak directly to the obstacles in your life, commanding them to align with God's will.

Barriers to Moving Mountains: Fear, Doubt, and Hesitation

Even with the promise of mountain-moving faith, many of us struggle to see results. Why? Because fear, doubt, and hesitation often paralyze our belief.

1. **Fear:** The enemy uses fear to magnify the size of the mountain and minimize God's power. Fear says, "What if I fail?" or "What if this is too big for God?"

2. **Doubt:** Doubt questions God's promises and undermines our confidence. Like Peter sinking in the water, doubt causes us to waver when we take our eyes off Jesus.

3. **Hesitation:** Sometimes, we simply fail to act. We wait for perfect conditions or greater assurance, forgetting that faith often requires stepping out before we see results.

The antidote to these barriers is to focus on God's faithfulness rather than the size of the mountain. As you meditate on His promises and take small steps of obedience, fear and doubt will lose their grip.

Personal Testimonies: Examples of Miraculous Breakthroughs

Faith that moves mountains isn't just a Biblical concept. It's alive and active today. Here are a few stories of transformation that illustrate this truth:

1. **Healing in Action:** A woman battling a terminal illness declared God's promises of healing daily. Against all odds, her body began to recover, baffling doctors. She attributes her healing to the power of faith-filled declarations and prayer.

2. **Financial Breakthrough:** A man facing bankruptcy prayed boldly, trusting God as his provider. Unexpectedly, opportunities and resources came his way, allowing him not only to recover but to prosper.

3. **Family Restoration:** A mother prayed for her estranged son, speaking life and reconciliation over their relationship. After years of silence, her son returned home, transformed by God's grace.

These testimonies remind us that faith isn't limited by time, place, or circumstance. God is still in the business of moving mountains.

How to Start Small: Building Your Faith to Face Greater Challenges

Mountain-moving faith doesn't happen overnight. Just as muscles grow through consistent exercise, faith strengthens as we use it in small, daily ways.

Here are practical steps to build your faith:

1. **Start with Small Mountains:** Begin by trusting God in manageable situations such as praying for favor at work or believing for healing in a minor illness. As you see God's faithfulness in these areas, your faith will grow for larger challenges.

2. **Keep a Faith Journal:** Record your prayers and the ways God answers them. This will serve as a testimony to His faithfulness when new challenges arise.

3. **Surround Yourself with Faith-Builders:** Spend time with people who inspire and encourage your faith. Avoid voices of negativity and doubt.

4. **Meditate on God's Promises:** Fill your heart and mind with Scriptures about God's power and faithfulness. The more you know His Word, the easier it is to trust Him.

Speak to Your Mountain

Faith that moves mountains is not reserved for the spiritually elite, it is available to anyone who believes. When you activate your faith through bold declarations, overcome the barriers of fear and doubt, and trust God's promises, you will see the impossible become possible.

Mountains will rise in your life, but with faith that transforms, you can command them to move. The question is, will you speak to your mountain today?

As you reflect on the mountains in your life, remember that faith is not about your ability to move them but about trusting the One who can. Surrender your obstacles to God, take steps of obedience, and trust that He is working, even when you can't see the results. Faith is a journey, not a one-time event. It requires continual trust, active declarations, and persistent action. The mountains in your life may appear immovable, but with God, nothing is impossible. Start where you are, speak to the obstacles in your path, and watch as God's power brings transformation. Remember, the greatness of your faith lies in the greatness of the God you serve.

Prayer:

Lord, thank You for the gift of faith. Help us to trust You more deeply and to align our lives with Your will. Give us the wisdom to act responsibly and the courage to believe that even the smallest faith can move mountains. May our lives reflect Your power and bring glory to Your name. Amen.

Returning What Doesn't Fit

Have you ever found yourself standing in the Return Line at a store, holding an item that didn't fit or wasn't what you wanted? It's a process we all know, waiting patiently, receipt in hand, ready to exchange what didn't work for something better. Faith, much like that return process, requires us to let go of what no longer serves us. It calls us to return the regrets, fears, and doubts that weigh us down so that God can exchange them for His promises, peace, and purpose.

But how often do we cling to what doesn't fit, convinced that it's too late to exchange it? Today, let's explore how faith allows us to return what doesn't work and trust God for something better.

The Bible Story: The Woman at the Well (John 4:1-30)

In John 4, we meet a Samaritan woman who came to a well at midday to draw water. Her life was filled with brokenness and shame; she had been married five times and was living with a man who wasn't her husband. Her trips to the well symbolized her attempt to satisfy a deeper thirst, one that no earthly solution could quench.

When Jesus met her, He invited her to return what wasn't working in her life, her failed relationships, her shame, her doubts, and exchange them for living water. He said, "Whoever drinks the water I give them will never thirst. Indeed, the water I give them will become in them a spring of water welling up to eternal life" (John 4:14).

The woman's faith led her to leave behind her jar, a symbol of her old way of life, and run to tell her community about Jesus. Her faith allowed her to exchange her brokenness for a new identity, her shame for joy, and her doubts for a testimony of transformation.

The Circle of Faith

Faith has a way of bringing things full circle. Like the Samaritan woman, it takes us from brokenness to restoration. It helps us put life into perspective, bringing order to the chaos and clarity to confusion. Doubt and fear, however, do the opposite, they disorient us, distract us from God, and keep us stuck in cycles of regret and self-doubt.

Faith asks:

➢ *Is this working for you?*
➢ *Does holding on to this regret, fear, or shame fit the life God has designed for you?*

God's answer is always the same: Return what doesn't fit. Like a loving Father, He wants us to bring Him what no longer has value in our lives, our mistakes, disappointments, and failures, so He can exchange them for something better.

Biblical Truths to Remember

1. **Faith Requires Surrender:** The Bible says, "Cast all your anxiety on Him because He cares for you" (1 Peter 5:7). Faith means trusting God enough to let go of what burdens us.

2. **God is a God of Exchange:** Isaiah 61:3 promises that God will give us "beauty for ashes, the oil of joy for mourning, the garment of praise for the spirit of heaviness." What we give up pales in comparison to what He gives in return.

3. **Faith Brings Order to Chaos:** "God is not a God of disorder but of peace" (1 Corinthians 14:33). Faith helps us put our lives into God's divine order, restoring peace and purpose.

What Are You Still Holding On To?

At some point this week, maybe when you're alone in your room, sitting in traffic, or even in the quiet of a bathroom stall, pause and ask yourself a holy, gut-level question: What am I holding on to that no longer fits the life God has for me? Be real. No filters. No excuses. Just you, God, and the truth. Is it fear? Shame? A toxic mindset? A relationship, a habit, a belief that keeps whispering, "You'll never change"?

Whatever it is, bring it into the light. Write it down if you have to. Name it. And then surrender it, fully, honestly, completely, before the Lord in prayer.

> Because here's the truth: God never asks you to let go without offering something better in return.

When you release what's been weighing you down, God fills that empty space with peace that steadies you, joy that revives you, and purpose that sets your soul on fire.

So don't wait. Don't carry it another day. Let God exchange what's broken for what's eternal.

You'll breathe easier. You'll walk lighter. And you'll step more fully into the life you were always meant to live.

God Exchanges What Doesn't Fit Our New Life in Christ

Faith is not just about letting go; it's about trusting God to replace the old with something new. When we surrender the things that no longer please God or align with our new life in Christ, He gives us something far greater in return.

The Apostle Paul reminds us in 2 Corinthians 5:17: "Therefore, if anyone is in Christ, the new creation has come: The old has gone, the new is here!" When we step into our new identity as followers of Christ, there are things from our old life that simply don't fit anymore, habits, mindsets, relationships, or even goals that are rooted in fear or selfish ambition. God calls us to exchange these things for the fruits of the Spirit (Galatians 5:22-23) and a purpose that reflects His kingdom.

Just like the Samaritan woman, who left behind her jar at the well, faith calls us to leave behind anything that hinders our walk with Christ. In return, God fills us with His Spirit, giving us peace, joy, and strength to live out our new life in Him.

In closing reflection, Faith is the return line of life, it's where we exchange what doesn't fit for what God has prepared for us. Just like the Samaritan woman, we all have jars we need to leave behind. When we come to God in faith, He doesn't just meet our needs; He exceeds them. Are you ready to return what's no longer working and receive the joy, peace, and purpose God has for you? Step out in faith and let Him transform your journey.

Prayer

Heavenly Father,

In You, I placed my trust.

Thank You for being a God of exchange. Today, I bring to You the things in my life that no longer fit, the regrets, the fears, the doubts, and the shame. I surrender them to You, knowing that You have something far better in store. Teach me O Lord, to trust You completely and to walk in faith, even when I don't see the full picture. Fill me with Your peace and renew my spirit with Your living water. Thank You for always meeting me where I am and for leading me to the life You've designed for me. In Jesus' name, I pray. Amen.

"Trust is the soil where faith takes root and the Spirit moves, transforming what you surrender into what God strengthens."

"Trust in the Lord with all your heart and lean not on your own understanding."
— Proverbs 3:5 (NIV)

Chapter 4:
THE TRANSFORMATIVE POWER OF TRUST

Faith That Transforms: Trust in Action

Transformative faith is more than belief; it is trust in action. Belief acknowledges God's existence and power, but trust goes further: it surrenders, obeys, and walks forward even when the way is unclear. Trust is the living bridge between intellectual agreement and wholehearted devotion, where faith moves from theory into reality. It's where faith takes root, anchoring us in God's promises and producing lasting fruit in our character, our decisions, and our relationships.

Why Trust Matters

Why is trust so vital? Because it's the application of faith when life gets real. It's one thing to say we believe God is good, sovereign, and wise; it's another to obey Him when He calls us into uncertainty, pain, or discomfort. Trust is faith with feet. Without trust, belief stays cerebral, sincere perhaps, but static. With trust, faith becomes dynamic, it speaks, moves, risks, and transforms.

> *Trust is not tested in comfort; it's revealed in crisis.*

When God calls us to forgive someone who has wounded us, to give when we feel stretched, or to step into a role we feel unqualified for,

that's where trust is forged. It's the difference between nodding at a truth and staking your life on it.

Trust Transforms Through Surrender

Trust transforms because it's grounded in surrender. It requires us to let go of control over our plans, outcomes, timelines, and fears, and place them in God's hands. But surrender doesn't come naturally. Our flesh craves certainty. We're drawn to the visible, the explainable, the predictable. And yet, spiritual growth happens when we loosen our grip and entrust the unknown to the One who knows all.

Consider Abraham, who left everything familiar because God said, "Go." He had no map, just a promise. Or Peter, who stepped onto a stormy sea at Jesus' invitation. Logic said stay in the boat, but trust said walk. And then there's the blind man in John 9. Jesus made mud from spit, placed it on his eyes, and told him to wash in a distant pool. The command was strange. The outcome was uncertain. But the man obeyed and was healed.

These moments weren't just expressions of belief; they were acts of radical trust. And that trust became the turning point for transformation.

Living a Trust-Fueled Faith

So what does this look like for us today?

> ➢ It's choosing peace when fear seems more natural.
> ➢ It's stepping into ministry when your qualifications feel small.
> ➢ It's releasing a relationship, dream, or outcome you've held tightly.
> ➢ It's saying "yes" to God before you see the full picture.

Trust turns belief into movement. It's not passive, it's a daily decision to lean into God's wisdom instead of your own, to follow His voice even when it challenges your comfort or defies human logic.

The Faith That Moves

Faith that transforms doesn't just acknowledge God; it yields to Him. It doesn't just agree with truth; it responds to it. Trust is where belief becomes embodied, where theology becomes lived experience. It's not easy. But it is worth it.

Because when we trust Him, really, trust Him, we don't just survive. We grow, we change, and we become living testimonies of what God can do with a surrendered life.

Trust Embraces God's Timing

One of the most challenging, and transformative, aspects of trust is learning to wait on God's timing. What feels like delay to us is often divine precision. God is never late; He is always working behind the scenes, shaping outcomes and refining us in the process. Trust teaches us to be patient, reminding us that God's plans rarely unfold on our timeline, but always according to His perfect wisdom.

In a culture addicted to immediacy, waiting can feel like failure or punishment. But biblically, waiting is a place of deep spiritual formation. It's in the waiting that God stretches our faith, strengthens our character, and prepares us for what's ahead. As Isaiah 40:31 promises:

> *"Those who wait on the Lord will renew their strength; they will soar on wings like eagles; they will run and not grow weary; they will walk and not faint."*

Waiting isn't passive, it's active trust. It is choosing to remain steady, to pray faithfully, and to obey fully, even when there's no visible sign of breakthrough. That kind of trust changes us from the inside out.

Lessons from Scripture and Real Life

We see this kind of trust modeled vividly in Scripture. Joseph endured betrayal, slavery, and imprisonment, not for days or weeks,

but for years. Yet through it all, he remained faithful, trusting that God was sovereign even in suffering. He didn't waste his waiting; he interpreted dreams, served with integrity, and gave God glory in a place that seemed forgotten. In time, God elevated him, but not before preparing him.

Esther, too, faced a pivotal moment that required bold trust. She risked her life to intervene for her people, believing that perhaps she had been positioned by God "for such a time as this" (Esther 4:14). Her courage didn't come from circumstance; it came from confidence in God's providence.

These stories remind us that trust isn't theoretical. It's gritty, real, and often forged in fire. Trust is the posture of the heart that says, "Even here, even now, I believe You're working."

Cultivating Trust in Everyday Life

But how do we cultivate this kind of trust in our own lives?

It begins with prayer, honest, ongoing dialogue with God. Trust grows as we bring our questions, fears, and longings to Him, not just once but continually. Prayer builds intimacy, reminding us that He is not only Sovereign, but personal, our Father, our Shepherd, our Friend.

We also nurture trust by immersing ourselves in Scripture. God's Word tells the long, faithful story of a God who never breaks His promises. It reminds us that He is trustworthy not just in theory, but in history.

Community is another essential element. We need people around us who will speak truth when we're discouraged, pray when we feel weak, and call us back to trust when we're tempted to doubt.

And most importantly, trust is built through obedience, small, consistent steps forward, even when the path is unclear. Whether it's forgiving someone who hurt you, stepping out into a new calling,

or choosing peace in the midst of chaos, every act of obedience is a declaration: "I trust You, Lord."

Final Thought: A Life Anchored in Trust

Trust is not a feeling we wait for; it's a decision we make. And as we learn to wait on God's timing, follow His leading, and obey His voice, trust becomes more than a concept. It becomes a way of life.

This is the kind of trust that transforms, not overnight, but over time. It's the trust that anchors us in storms, strengthens us in waiting, and positions us to experience the fullness of God's faithfulness.

Trust is the active ingredient that transforms faith into a life-changing force. It moves us beyond believing *about* God to living *for* Him, surrendering our plans and fears into His hands. When we step forward in trust, whether through bold obedience or patient waiting, we position ourselves for God's greatest work in and through us. Trusting God isn't always easy, but it is always worth it.

Surrendering to Transformation

Trust is the bridge between faith and transformation. It is the daily act of surrendering our will to God, believing that His plans are better than ours. When we trust God, whether by stepping forward in bold obedience or waiting patiently in seasons of silence, He uses that trust to refine us and bring about His purposes in our lives.

As you surrender control and lean into God's faithfulness, you'll discover that trust doesn't just change your circumstances, it changes you. Faith transforms, but trust completes the work. Will you take the leap today?

In *Walking on Holy Ground: Faith That Transforms*, discover the life-changing power of faith. Just as Moses was called to remove his sandals and stand before God, you are invited to cast off the 'shoes' of pride, fear, and distractions that hinder your journey.

Walking on Holy Ground

Faith allows us to enter into the very presence of God. When Moses approached the burning bush, God commanded him not to come any closer and to take off his sandals because he was standing on holy ground (Exodus 3:5). What do the sandals represent? They symbolize the things of the world, the dust, distractions, and sin that cling to our daily lives. Removing them is a metaphor for surrender, reverence, and the preparation of the heart to encounter God. Just as Moses stood in awe of God's presence, so too must we remove anything that hinders our walk with Him. Faith invites us into this sacred space, transforming our lives and drawing us closer to His glory.

Faith is more than belief; it is an invitation into a sacred space where transformation begins and where we are drawn closer to the fullness of God's glory. It is not a passive state but an active relationship, a profound encounter that reshapes our hearts, minds, and lives. Faith invites us to step beyond the ordinary and into the extraordinary, to enter into the holy presence of God, where we are changed, renewed, and empowered to reflect His glory in our lives.

When we enter into this sacred place, we are protected by His supernatural presence and His glory. The Presence of God is not merely a comforting idea; it is a transformative reality that brings true joy and satisfaction. King David captured this beautifully in Psalm 16:11: "You make known to me the path of life; in your presence there is fullness of joy; at your right hand are pleasures forevermore." In His presence, we discover the joy that surpasses any earthly pleasure and the satisfaction that can only be found in Him. Your soul was made for God, and it is only in His presence that it finds its true home.

Consider the story of Moses a little bit further, a man who experienced the tangible presence of God in ways that still leave us in awe. When Moses stood before the burning bush, he encountered God not as an abstract idea but as the Living One, calling him to a divine mission. This moment of faith required Moses to trust God beyond his insecurities and limitations. He was drawn into the sacred space

where human frailty meets divine purpose, and his life was forever transformed. Faith allows us to be in the holy presence of God himself. Glory be to God! Yet, it also requires us to spiritually remove the sandals of the world. Whatever hinders us from being in God's presence.

Later, on Mount Sinai, Moses entered an even deeper encounter with God. He stood in the thick cloud of His presence, receiving the Law and beholding God's glory in a way that left his face radiant, a reflection so powerful that it had to be veiled. This moment reveals something profound: being in the presence of God transforms us. It illuminates, purifies us, and lifts us up, aligning our hearts with His will and filling us with His light. It is in this sacred space, this holy communion, that we are no longer defined by our weaknesses but by His strength and glory working in us.

Faith is the doorway to this sacred space. It is what draws us into the presence of God, not merely to receive blessings, but to be changed by Him. Like Moses, we are invited to climb the mountain, to leave behind the noise and distractions of the world, and to stand face-to-face with the One who is holy, loving, and sovereign. In His presence, our fears are quieted, our doubts are silenced, and our hearts are reoriented toward His purpose.

The presence of God is not only transformative; it is life-giving. It is here that we find the fullness of joy, the satisfaction for which our souls were created. This is where faith leads us, not just to believe in God but to draw near to Him, to dwell in His glory, and to live lives that reflect the radiant beauty of His love and power.

The "Shoes" of the World God Wants Us to Remove

When God told Moses to remove his sandals on holy ground (Exodus 3:5), it symbolized a shedding of worldly attachments, impurities, and anything unworthy of God's presence. Today, God calls us to remove the metaphorical "shoes" of the world, things that hinder our relationship with Him and our ability to reflect His glory.

Here's a list of some of the "shoes" God wants us to remove:

1. **Hatred:** The opposite of God's love. Hatred poisons our hearts and relationships (1 John 4:20).

2. **Pride:** Pride keeps us from fully surrendering to God. "God opposes the proud but gives grace to the humble" (James 4:6).

3. **Dishonesty:** A lack of integrity disrupts our witness and separates us from God's truth (Proverbs 12:22).

4. **Bitterness:** Holding grudges or unforgiveness blocks the flow of God's grace in our lives (Ephesians 4:31-32).

5. **Greed:** The pursuit of worldly wealth and possessions distracts us from seeking God's kingdom first (Matthew 6:33).

6. **Fear and Anxiety:** Fear undermines faith, while God calls us to trust Him completely (2 Timothy 1:7).

7. **Selfish Ambition**: Seeking our own gain instead of serving others is contrary to Christ's example of humility (Philippians 2:3-4).

8. **Lust:** Craving what is not ours corrupts the purity of our hearts (1 Thessalonians 4:3-5).

9. **Resentment:** Harboring past wounds instead of laying them at God's feet prevents healing and freedom (Colossians 3:13).

10. **Idolatry:** Placing anything, work, relationships, success, above God in our hearts distances us from His glory (Exodus 20:3).

Each of these "shoes" reflects worldly thinking, but when removed, they make room for God's Spirit to work in us, transforming us into His image. Our question becomes what shoes are we wearing as believers of Christ?

How Faith Leads Us Into a Life Transformed by His Glory

Faith is the foundation for transformation. It is through faith that we lay down the things of the world and take up the promises of God.

Faith enables us to see beyond our circumstances and trust in the unseen (Hebrews 11:1).

Here are ways faith leads us to transformation:

1. Faith Opens the Door to God's Presence

Faith grants us access to God's presence, where transformation begins. Just as Moses stepped onto holy ground, we must approach God with reverence and expectation, believing He will meet us where we are.

"Let us then approach God's throne of grace with confidence, so that we may receive mercy and find grace to help us in our time of need" (Hebrews 4:16).

2. Faith Enables Surrender

Through faith, we lay down our pride, fears, and worldly attachments, trusting that God's plans are higher than ours. Surrender allows God to refine us and fill us with His Spirit.

"Trust in the Lord with all your heart and lean not on your own understanding" (Proverbs 3:5).

3. Faith Aligns Us with God's Will

Faith leads us to obedience. As we trust God's Word and follow His commands, we align ourselves with His purpose. This alignment allows His glory to flow through our lives. "If you remain in me and I in you, you will bear much fruit" (John 15:5).

4. Faith Transforms Our Minds and Hearts

Faith renews our thinking, replacing worldly desires with godly values. It softens our hearts to be compassionate, forgiving, and full of love. "Do not conform to the pattern of this world, but be transformed by the renewing of your mind" (Romans 12:2).

5. Faith Produces Endurance and Maturity

Trials often challenge our faith, but they also strengthen it. Through perseverance, God shapes our character and prepares us for greater works of His glory. "Consider it pure joy... whenever you face trials... because you know that the testing of your faith produces perseverance" (James 1:2-3).

6. Faith Reflects God's Glory

As we grow in faith, we reflect God's character to the world. His love, grace, and power shine through us, making us living testimonies of His glory. "In the same way, let your light shine before others, that they may see your good deeds and glorify your Father in heaven" (Matthew 5:16).

Steps Toward Transformation by Faith

1. Confess and Remove Worldly Shoes

Examine your heart and identify the "shoes" of the world you are still wearing. Pray for God to reveal and help you remove them.

2. Spend Time in God's Word

Faith comes by hearing and meditating on God's Word (Romans 10:17). Scripture renews your mind and anchors you in truth.

3. Pray with Expectation

Approach God in faith, believing He hears your prayers and desires to transform you.

4. Walk in Obedience

Faith without action is dead (James 2:17). Take steps to obey God, even when it feels uncomfortable.

5. Seek God's Presence Daily

Make worship, prayer, and fellowship with God a priority. Transformation happens in His presence.

6. Trust the Process

God's transformation is not instant but continuous. Trust Him to complete the good work He started in you (Philippians 1:6).

What Is God's Glory?

Have you ever asked yourself, *what is God's glory?* It is more than light or beauty, it is the manifestation of His holiness, power, and presence. God's glory is His very essence revealed.

Psalm 24:1 declares, "The earth is the Lord's, and the fullness thereof," meaning that all creation reflects His glory. The vastness of the skies, the majesty of the mountains, the intricate details of a flower, all point to a Creator who is infinite in wisdom and power. Yet, God's greatest reflection of glory is found in *you,* His creation, made in His image (Genesis 1:27).

When God is at the center of your life, His glory radiates from within, transforming you from the inside out. But how do you carry His presence and live under His favor? How do you know when the glory of God rests upon you?

Faith: The Key to God's Presence

Faith is the doorway into God's glory.

Hebrews 11:6 reminds us, "Without faith it is impossible to please God." Faith requires trusting God even when circumstances seem bleak.

Imagine being in a place of despair, losing a job, facing heartbreak, or grappling with guilt over past mistakes. These moments often feel

like the end of the road. Yet, they are opportunities to encounter God's glory. Like Moses standing before the burning bush, you are on holy ground. In those moments, God invites you to surrender, listen, and trust Him.

Faith removes the "shoes" of pride, fear, and worldly distractions that separate us from God's presence. It prepares us to experience His transformative power.

The Longing for God's Glory

David, a man after God's own heart, expressed a deep hunger for God's presence. In Psalm 27:4, he wrote, "One thing I ask from the Lord, this only do I seek: that I may dwell in the house of the Lord all the days of my life, to gaze on the beauty of the Lord and to seek him in his temple."

David's longing wasn't for material blessings or fleeting joys—it was for the very presence of God. This same desire should fuel our hearts today. When we seek God, we aren't just asking for His hand of provision; we are seeking His face, His glory, and His transforming presence.

The Transforming Power of God's Glory

The Apostle Paul wrote in 2 Corinthians 3:18, "We all, who with unveiled faces contemplate the Lord's glory, are being transformed into His image with ever-increasing glory, which comes from the Lord, who is the Spirit."

This transformation is not a one-time event but a lifelong process. When we encounter God's glory, it changes us. It refines our character, softens our hearts, and renews our minds. We begin to reflect His love, grace, and power to the world around us.

Take a moment to reflect: Are you being transformed by His glory? Are you allowing His Spirit to work in every area of your life?

Surrender: The Path to Glory

Jesus prayed in John 17:22, "I have given them the glory that you gave me, that they may be one as we are one." This glory is not something we earn; it is a gift freely given to those who abide in Christ.

To receive this glory, we must surrender. Surrender means letting go of our desires, our plans, and our pride. It means taking up our cross daily (Luke 9:23) and aligning our lives with God's will.

Like Moses, we must remove our "shoes" and stand in reverence before God. In doing so, we position ourselves to encounter His presence and be transformed by His glory.

The World's Distractions vs. God's Glory

The world offers countless distractions that compete for our attention. Social media, materialism, and busyness can pull us away from God's presence. But nothing compares to the beauty of knowing Him.

Isaiah 40:28 reminds us, "The Lord is the everlasting God, the Creator of the ends of the earth. He will not grow tired or weary, and his understanding no one can fathom." His glory is eternal, unchanging, and far greater than anything the world can offer.

Holy Ground: What Does It Mean?

When God told Moses, "Take off your sandals, for the place where you are standing is holy ground" (Exodus 3:5), He was emphasizing the sacredness of His presence. Holy ground is not about the physical location; it is about the presence of God.

Wherever you encounter God, whether in a church, in your home, or during a moment of prayer, that place becomes holy ground. It is where heaven touches earth, where God's glory meets humanity.

In closing reflections, God's glory is not a distant concept; it is a tangible reality available to all who seek Him. As you surrender to

Him and walk by faith, you will encounter His presence in ways that transform your life.

Faith is not passive; it's active and transformational. It moves us from a life burdened by the "shoes" of the world to a life of freedom, joy, and purpose in God's presence. As you walk by faith, His glory will rest upon you, transforming you into His likeness.

Just as God called Moses to holy ground, He is calling you today. Take off your "shoes," step into His presence, and allow your faith to lead you into a life transformed by His glory. As we cast off the "shoes" of the world and walk in obedience, we step into the fullness of His presence with a thankful heart and purpose. Will you take off your sandals today and step boldly into a life transformed by His glory?

A Prayer for Transformation by Faith

Heavenly Father,

Thank You for calling us into Your holy presence. Help us to remove the "shoes" of this world, hatred, pride, fear, and all that separates us from You. Strengthen our faith to trust in Your plans and promises. Transform our hearts and minds to reflect Your glory in every area of our lives.

Lord, we long to walk in the beauty of Your presence, to be changed daily by Your Spirit, and to live as vessels of Your love and grace. Teach us to surrender fully and to seek Your will above all else. May our lives be living testimonies of Your power and faithfulness.

Even now, Lord God, we thank You for inviting us into Your Holy presence and allowing us to experience Your glory. Faith tells that we are worthy. Teach us to walk boldly by faith, to surrender our fears and distractions, and to seek You above all else. Lord, we long to stand on holy ground, to encounter You in a deeper way, and to be transformed by Your Spirit. May Your glory shine through us, reflecting Your love and grace to a world in need. Draw us closer to You each day and help us to live lives that honor and glorify Your name.

In Jesus' name, we pray. Amen.

"Faith is the master key; when turned in full trust, it unlocks the weight of God's power and the authority of His name."

"Behold, I give you authority... over all the power of the enemy, and nothing shall by any means hurt you." — Luke 10:19 (NKJV)

Chapter 5:

FAITH AS THE DIVINE CONNECTOR

What if faith is more than belief, more than a principle, more than a pillar of religion or a word whispered in desperate prayer?

> What if faith is the sacred thread that ties the human heart to the throne of God?

What if it is heaven's language, the heartbeat of the Spirit, the bridge that carries you from the wilderness of doubt into the glory of divine encounter?

Within the depths of our inner selves, there exists a yearning for greater fulfillment. Not more religion. Not more routine. But more of God, more presence, more power, more transformation. We crave something eternal to awaken within us. Something real. Something holy. Something that breathes life where we've only known survival. And it is faith, living, breathing, dynamic faith that leads us there.

Why Faith? Why Now?

Faith is not an option in the Christian life, it is the foundation, the fuel, and the fire. It is the language of heaven and the Divine Connector between a holy God and a seeking soul. Faith is how we hear God, how we respond, how we access His presence, and how we partner with Him in our purpose. Hebrews 11:6 tells us plainly:

"Without faith, it is impossible to please God." Not difficult. Not unlikely. Impossible.

And yet, faith is not passive. It's not polite. It's not tidy. Faith moves. It shouts. It breaks chains. It walks on water. It believes when the world mocks belief. It defies logic. It refuses to be confined. Faith is not a quiet inner strength; it is the roar of heaven breaking into the chaos of earth.

Faith: Heaven's Touchpoint on Earth

Picture it: your soul, like a switch waiting to be flipped. Faith is the ignition. It turns on everything heaven has stored up for your life. It opens the vault of God's promises. It releases His kingdom into your reality. Through faith, you don't just hear about God's love, you live in it. You don't just wish for peace; you carry it into chaos. You don't just wait for purpose; you walk in it boldly.

That's why Jesus said, "Your faith has made you well." Not your education. Not your background. Not your perfection. Your faith. God responds to faith. Not the size of it, but the surrender behind it.

> Faith isn't about control; it's about trust. It's the posture of the soul that says, "God, I believe You more than I believe what I see."

Faith Transforms Because It Touches Eternity

Faith doesn't just change your situation, it changes you. It's how God rewires your mind, rebuilds your heart, and renews your vision. Romans 12:2 speaks of a transformation that begins with the renewing of the mind. And faith is the spark that ignites it.

Think of Abraham, walking away from everything familiar because God said, "Go." Think of Moses, trembling before a bush that burned with holy fire, barefoot and overwhelmed, but willing. Think of Peter, eyes locked on Jesus, stepping out onto stormy waters. Their faith didn't just move mountains; it shaped the story of redemption.

And that same Spirit, the same resurrection power, lives in you.

Faith Aligns Us with God's Nature and Glory

Faith isn't magic. It's alignment. It's how we come into agreement with who God is and what He's doing. When we live by faith, we begin to think God's thoughts, walk in His ways, and carry His heart into every corner of our world.

Moses didn't just ask to see God's glory, he carried it. His face radiated the very presence of God. That's what faith does. It makes us mirrors of the divine. It takes ordinary people and turns them into vessels of holiness, fire, and transformation.

Faith Shapes a Life of Eternal Purpose

God doesn't just have plans for your life; He has a divine blueprint marked by destiny. Jeremiah 29:11 is not wishful thinking; it's a promise sealed in the heart of God. But it's faith that unlocks it. Faith doesn't just help you discover your purpose; it gives you the boldness to live it.

Think of Mary. Her yes to God birthed the Savior. Think of Paul. His surrender sparked a revolution that still echoes in the Church today. Faith doesn't just write personal success stories; it writes kingdom stories. And God is still writing them, through people like you.

Faith: The Engine of God's Glory

Faith is the delivery system of God's glory into your life. It doesn't promise ease, but it guarantees transformation. It doesn't take away the fire, but it gives you the strength to walk through it and come out glowing. It doesn't eliminate the valley, but it assures you that you're never alone in it.

So the real question isn't, "Do you have enough faith?" The question is, "Are you willing to activate the faith you already have?" Jesus said

even mustard-seed faith can move mountains. Even trembling faith can reach out and touch the hem of His garment, and receive healing.

You weren't created to live a life of safe, stagnant belief. You were made for more, for fire, for faith, for the fullness of God's glory in you.

Faith as the Bridge Between God's Promises and Fulfillment

Faith is the mechanism that unlocks God's power, connects us to His authority, and accomplishes His divine purpose. When released in obedience and alignment with God's will, faith transforms the unseen promises of God into tangible reality. Like a remote control that activates the full potential of a television, faith is the divine connector that bridges the gap between what God has spoken and its manifestation in our lives.

By embracing and releasing this dynamic force, believers can experience the fullness of God's power, authority, and purpose in their journey of faith.

As we examine this concept of faith aligning with God's will, we can indeed draw parallels to the analogy of a remote control operating a television. Faith, like the remote control, functions as a connector and activator between us and God's power, releasing divine action when aligned with His purpose. Let's explore this comparison in more depth while also diving into the transformative and unlocking power of faith.

Comparison: Faith and a TV Remote Control

1. Purpose and Intent

* Remote Control: When you pick up a remote and point it at the TV, your intent is clear, you want the TV to respond by turning on, changing the channel, or performing a specific function.

- Faith: Similarly, when faith is released, its purpose is intentional, it is aimed at aligning with God's will to achieve His divine plans. Faith is not random; it is purposeful, activated to accomplish what God has already spoken.

2. Activation and Action

- Remote Control: Pressing a button releases a signal that activates the TV to perform a task. The remote doesn't work on its own but must be used in conjunction with the TV, which is the source of its operation.

- Faith: Releasing faith involves active participation, prayer, obedience, and trust. Faith doesn't act independently but draws its power from God. When activated, it releases God's authority and promises to manifest His will in the situation.

3. Alignment

- Remote Control: For the remote to work, it must be properly aligned and pointed toward the TV. Misalignment means the signal won't reach its target.

- Faith: For faith to work, it must be aligned with God's will. Misplaced or self-focused faith (e.g., trying to use faith for selfish desires) will not achieve God's purposes. True faith operates within the boundaries of God's promises and plans.

4. Invisible Power

- Remote Control: Though the signal between the remote and TV is invisible, the results are evident once the TV responds.

- Faith: Faith operates in a similar way, it is unseen, yet its results become tangible as God's power and authority are released to transform situations and accomplish His will.

Faith That Unlocks God's Power and Authority

Faith serves as the mechanism that unlocks God's power and activates His promises in our lives. When released, faith aligns with God's divine purpose and brings transformation, just as the remote signals the TV to fulfill its intended functions.

1. Faith Transforms

➢ Faith is not passive; it is a transformative force. It changes situations, hearts, and lives by inviting God's power into circumstances. For example:

- *Healing*: The woman with the issue of blood (Mark 5:25-34) released her faith when she touched Jesus' garment, believing she would be healed. Her faith unlocked the transformative power of God.
- *Provision*: Faith activated the multiplication of loaves and fish (Matthew 14:13-21) when Jesus blessed the small offering.

2. Faith Unlocks Authority

➢ Faith taps into God's authority, enabling believers to act with boldness and assurance. Jesus emphasized this in Matthew 17:20 when He said faith as small as a mustard seed could move mountains.

➢ This is not because of the size of faith but because of its connection to God's unlimited power. Faith released in alignment with God's will becomes the conduit through which His authority operates in the world.

3. Faith Accomplishes Divine Purpose

➢ Isaiah 55:11 says God's Word does not return void but accomplishes His purpose. When faith is directed toward God's Word, it aligns with this principle.

➢ Faith acts as a delivery mechanism, ensuring that God's promises come to fruition. For instance:

- Noah's faith in God's Word led him to build the ark, fulfilling God's purpose of preservation.

- Abraham's faith in God's promise of a son resulted in Isaac's birth and the fulfillment of God's covenant.

In conclusion, Faith transforms and unlocks the authority of God when it is released in alignment with His will. It is the active force that bridges the gap between the invisible promises of God and their tangible fulfillment in our lives. Faith acts as a bridge between God and His people. It's the means by which believers access His power, align with His nature, and live out His purpose for their lives.

Grace plays a foundational and inseparable role in the concept of faith as the dynamic force that unlocks God's power and authority. Faith cannot operate effectively without grace, as grace is both the source and the sustaining power behind faith. Let's explore the relationship between grace and faith and how grace shapes and empowers this dynamic process:

Faith is the Gift of Grace

1. Grace as the Origin of Faith

➤ Faith is a Gift of Grace:
Ephesians 2:8-9 teaches that faith is a gift from God, given by His grace, not something we earn or achieve on our own. Without God's unmerited favor, we wouldn't even have the capacity to believe or trust Him.

➤ Implication: This means that the very ability to release faith begins with grace. God provides both the seed of faith and the opportunity to act upon it.

➤ Grace as the Foundation of Relationship:
Through grace, God initiates the relationship between Himself and humanity. Faith is our response to that grace, enabling us to trust His character, promises, and plans.

➢ Example: The call of Abraham to leave his homeland (Genesis 12:1-4) was an act of God's grace. Abraham's faith was his response to the grace that first reached out to him.

2. Grace Empowers the Release of Faith

➢ Grace Sustains Obedience in Faith:

Grace gives us the strength to act in obedience when releasing faith requires courage or sacrifice. It is by God's grace that we can endure trials, step out in trust, and align with His will.

➢ Example: Paul writes in 2 Corinthians 12:9, "My grace is sufficient for you, for my power is made perfect in weakness." Here, grace enables believers to move in faith even in their weakness.

➢ Grace Enables Access to God's Promises:

Faith unlocks God's promises, but grace ensures they are freely given, not earned. Romans 5:2 says, "Through Him, we have also obtained access by faith into this grace in which we stand."

➢ Implication: Grace creates the framework where faith operates, ensuring that God's promises are fulfilled as a result of His love and favor, not human effort or merit.

3. Grace and Alignment with God's Will

➢ Grace Aligns Our Hearts:

Faith requires alignment with God's will, and grace is what transforms our hearts and minds to desire His purpose over our own. Philippians 2:13 explains, "For it is God who works in you, both to will and to work for His good pleasure."

▪ Implication: Grace ensures that our faith is directed toward God's plans rather than selfish ambition, making our faith effective in accomplishing His purpose.

➢ Grace Overcomes Human Limitations:

In our natural state, we are incapable of fully understanding or aligning with God's will. Grace bridges the gap, giving us divine insight and strength to trust Him beyond what we can see or comprehend.

- Example: Mary's faith to accept the angel's announcement of Jesus' birth (Luke 1:38) was empowered by God's grace, which enabled her to align with a plan far beyond her understanding.

4. Grace Prevents Faith from Becoming Works-Based

➢ Faith Functions Through Grace, Not Effort:

There is a danger of viewing faith as something we "do" to earn God's power or promises. Grace ensures that faith remains a humble response to God's initiative, not a means of control or manipulation.

- Example: The Pharisees exhibited self-reliant works, but Jesus emphasized that faith must rest on God's grace and not human effort (Matthew 23:23).
- Key Thought: Faith operates through grace, ensuring that all glory goes to God, not to human effort or ability.

5. Grace Amplifies the Results of Faith

➢ **Grace & Faith — A Divine Partnership**

"And from His fullness we have all received, grace upon grace."
– John 1:16 (ESV)

When faith is exercised in alignment with God's will, grace does more than support it, it multiplies it. Grace doesn't just accompany faith; it amplifies its effect, elevating the outcome far beyond what human strength or strategy could ever accomplish.

Faith Activates, Grace Multiplies

Consider the miracle of the feeding of the 5,000 (John 6:1–14). A boy's humble offering, five loaves and two fish, was placed in Jesus' hands. Through a simple prayer of faith, He offered it to the Father. What followed was not mere addition, but miraculous multiplication.

This moment reveals a profound truth: when faith meets grace, heaven's resources are released. What we place in God's hands by faith is transformed by His grace into more than enough.

Grace Breaks Through Natural Limits

Grace ensures that the results of faith are not confined by human logic or natural law. It demonstrates the supernatural power of God, making what seems impossible a reality. Where we see limitation, grace sees opportunity.

> Grace Doesn't Just Change Circumstances, It Changes You

Grace isn't only external, it's deeply personal. It works in tandem with faith to refine us, reshape us, and restore us.

Take Peter, for example. Though he denied Christ, he was not disqualified. In John 21:15–19, we witness Jesus not condemning him, but restoring him by grace. Peter's journey, marked by both failure and faith, was sustained and ultimately fulfilled through God's grace.

The Synergy of Grace and Faith

Grace and faith are not two separate tracks, they are deeply intertwined. One fuels the other:

➢ Grace is the source.

➢ Faith is the response.

➢ Grace empowers.

➢ Faith releases.

➢ Grace sustains.

➢ Faith believes.

Together, they form a divine partnership that enables us not only to witness miracles, but to become living testimonies of God's transforming power.

Walk in Grace-Filled Faith

When we understand and embrace the role of grace in our faith walk, we shift from striving to abiding, from doubt to confidence, and from limitation to overflow. We stop leaning on our own ability and begin trusting in God's unmerited favor, a favor that guides, sustains, and amplifies the work He begins in us.

Let grace carry your faith, and watch God do the extraordinary through your ordinary.

Scripture for Reflection:

"But by the grace of God I am what I am, and his grace to me was not without effect. No, I worked harder than all of them—yet not I, but the grace of God that was with me."
– 1 Corinthians 15:10 (NIV)

Chapter 6:
LIVING OUT YOUR BELIEFS DAILY

In this chapter, we will explore how this kind of faith can revolutionize your perspective, elevate your actions, and draw you into a deeper, more intimate relationship with God. Together, we will discover how faith is not just a belief system but a dynamic force that touches every corner of your life, inspiring change in both you and the world around you.

Transformative faith is not limited to extraordinary moments of spiritual awakening or life-changing decisions. While those moments can serve as catalysts, true faith is a lifestyle, a daily, intentional commitment to align every aspect of your life with God's truth. It is about living out your beliefs consistently and authentically in the ordinary rhythms of life. Transformative faith isn't just something you experience in pivotal moments; it is woven into the fabric of your choices, habits, and interactions, making it a practical and tangible expression of your relationship with God.

True faith is inherently active, not passive. It shapes the way you think, speak, and act, guiding your decisions and influencing your priorities. For instance, faith prompts you to respond with kindness in situations where anger might feel justified, to extend forgiveness even when it is difficult, and to persevere when circumstances seem overwhelming. It inspires a mindset of humility and gratitude, driving you to put others' needs before your own. By living out your faith in these ways, you become a vessel through which God's love and truth can flow into the lives of those around you.

Transformative faith can redefine your everyday life.

It explores the ways faith inspires acts of love and service, turning mundane tasks into opportunities to glorify God and bless others. Whether it's through a simple word of encouragement, lending a helping hand, or showing compassion to someone in need, faith manifests itself in countless small but meaningful ways.

Moreover, faith is the foundation for continual spiritual growth. It keeps you rooted in God's promises, even when life feels uncertain, and encourages you to remain steadfast in your walk with Him. Transformative faith fuels a hunger for God's Word, deepens your prayer life, and cultivates a heart that seeks to obey Him in all things. Through this active, daily expression of faith, you not only grow closer to God but also become a living testimony of His power to transform hearts and lives.

Faith as a Lifestyle: Demonstrating Belief in Daily Choices

Faith is not merely a declaration or something you profess with your words; it is a way of life, demonstrated through your actions and decisions. How? True faith is alive and dynamic, influencing every aspect of your behavior and choices. It compels you to act in alignment with God's truth, making it evident not only in what you believe but in how you live. As James 2:26 states, "Faith without works is dead." This profound statement emphasizes that faith, when genuine, will always result in tangible expressions of obedience, love, and service.

It is important to recognize that this does not imply our actions result in salvation. Salvation is a gift from God, given by grace through faith (Ephesians 2:8-9). However, the works that flow from faith are the evidence of its authenticity. Genuine faith is transformative, it changes the way you see the world, your purpose, and your role in God's kingdom. When faith takes root in your heart, it naturally produces fruit, just as a healthy tree bears good fruit (Matthew 7:17).

Consider this: if you truly believe in God's promises, His goodness, and His call to love others, your actions will reflect that belief. Faith inspires you to forgive when it's difficult, to serve when it's inconvenient, and to trust God's plan even when it doesn't align with your own understanding. It is not a passive state of belief but an active partnership with God that compels you to embody His love and truth in your daily life.

James uses examples to illustrate this principle, such as Abraham, whose faith was made complete by his willingness to act on God's command, and Rahab, whose faith led her to protect the spies despite personal risk (James 2:21-25). These examples remind us that faith is not isolated from action; it is validated and made visible through it.

In practical terms, this means that faith calls you to move beyond words and step into action, whether by helping those in need, showing kindness to a stranger, or pursuing God's purposes with courage and perseverance. Faith without action is stagnant, but faith coupled with action transforms both the believer and the world around them.

In summary, faith and works are inseparable because they are two sides of the same coin. Works do not save us, but they reveal the life-changing power of faith at work within us. Genuine faith produces a lifestyle that reflects God's character, enabling us to live as His hands and feet in a world that desperately needs His love and grace.

Living out faith as a lifestyle means that your belief in God influences every area of your life: how you treat others, how you respond to challenges, and even how you use your time and resources. Faith that transforms isn't compartmentalized to Sundays or church activities, it touches your work, relationships, and the smallest choices of your day.

Every decision becomes an opportunity to express your trust in God. Do you act with integrity at work, even when no one is watching? Do you choose kindness when faced with someone difficult? Faith is demonstrated in these everyday moments.

Practical Expressions: Giving, Serving, and Loving as Acts of Faith

Faith finds its fullest expression in love. Galatians 5:6 declares, *"The only thing that counts is faith expressing itself through love."* Giving, serving, and loving others are not just good deeds; they are acts of faith that reflect God's heart and demonstrate trust in His provision.

1. **Giving:** Faith calls us to give generously, trusting that God will meet our needs. Whether it's tithing, supporting a cause, or helping someone in need, giving challenges us to let go of fear and embrace God's abundance.

2. **Serving**: Serving others requires humility and selflessness. When we volunteer our time or lend a helping hand, we live out the faith that values others above ourselves. Jesus Himself set the ultimate example when He washed His disciples' feet.

3. **Loving:** Faith transforms relationships. It calls us to love not just those who are easy to love but also our enemies.

> Love as an act of faith requires forgiveness, patience, and grace. It shows the world the transformative power of God's love.

Each of these actions demonstrates a faith that is alive and growing. When you give, serve, and love, you partner with God in transforming the world around you.

Overcoming Complacency: Staying Active in Your Spiritual Walk

One of the greatest obstacles to living out a vibrant and transformative faith is complacency. Complacency creeps in subtly, often disguised as comfort or routine, lulling us into a passive approach to our spiritual walk. When life feels steady and secure, it's easy to take our faith for granted, focusing on earthly pleasures or relying on our own strength rather than seeking God's presence and guidance. This stagnation is dangerous because faith, by its very nature, is designed

to grow, evolve, and deepen. When left unattended, it weakens, leaving us unprepared for life's inevitable trials.

But what happens when life is no longer comfortable? When the foundations of our comfort are shaken, whether by hardship, loss, or uncertainty, our need for God becomes undeniable. Yet, this is often when we realize how distant we've become, as if we've placed God on a shelf in the pantry, reserved for emergencies. We reach for Him only in desperation, forgetting that He desires a consistent, intimate relationship with us, not just a fleeting cry for help. Faith that transforms is not a tool for crisis management; it is a daily dependence on God, a commitment to prioritize Him in every season, whether in abundance or in adversity.

This kind of faith requires consistent growth, renewal, and active involvement with God. Transformation cannot happen if we remain passive in our pursuit of Him. Just as a plant needs water and sunlight to thrive, our faith requires nourishment through prayer, study of the Word, worship, and fellowship with other believers. It also demands self-reflection and humility, a willingness to recognize where complacency has taken root and to invite God to reignite our passion for Him.

God, in His infinite grace, gives all of Himself to us. He holds nothing back, offering His love, mercy, wisdom, and even His Spirit to dwell within us. Why, then, should we give Him anything less? Imagine the depth of relationship we could experience if we gave God the same unwavering commitment He gives us. He longs to be at the center of our lives, not pushed to the margins or reserved for moments of crisis.

To overcome complacency, we must choose daily to surrender to God and invite Him into every aspect of our lives. This requires intentionality, seeking Him in the ordinary and extraordinary, cultivating gratitude, and trusting Him even when life feels uncertain. When we offer ourselves fully to God, He renews our hearts, strengthens our faith, and equips us to navigate life's challenges with hope and purpose.

In essence, faith that transforms is not about convenience or comfort; it's about consistency and commitment. It calls us to move beyond passive belief into an active, living relationship with God. This is the kind of faith that not only sustains us but changes us, allowing us to reflect His glory and fulfill the purpose He has for our lives.

Complacency often creeps in when:

➢ You rely on past experiences of faith rather than seeking God daily.

➢ You avoid challenges that require you to step out of your comfort zone.

➢ You neglect spiritual disciplines, like prayer and Scripture reading.

To overcome complacency, intentionally seek opportunities to stretch your faith. Join a new ministry, mentor someone in their faith journey, or take on a challenge that forces you to rely on God. As you stay active in your spiritual walk, your faith will continue to deepen and transform you.

In conclusion, Faith that transforms begins with the small choices and consistent actions that reflect your trust in God. Living out your faith daily can be challenging, but it is also profoundly rewarding. Why? Because faith, when actively practiced, transforms not only your relationship with God but also your perspective on life, your interactions with others, and your ability to navigate trials with hope and purpose. While the path of faith is not without obstacles, the rewards far outweigh the difficulties, offering peace, joy, and fulfillment that nothing else can provide.

For example, living out your faith might mean choosing patience and kindness in a difficult relationship, even when it would be easier to respond with anger or indifference. It could involve trusting God with a decision that feels uncertain, believing His plan is greater than your fears. Or it might mean stepping out of your comfort zone to serve others, whether by helping a struggling neighbor, volunteering

your time, or offering a listening ear to someone in need. Each of these actions, though not always easy, brings a deep sense of purpose and connection to God's greater work in the world.

Another reward of living out your faith daily is the peace it brings, even in the face of adversity. For instance, when life feels overwhelming, prayer and reliance on God can calm your spirit, reminding you that you are not alone. This peace is not dependent on circumstances; it is rooted in the knowledge that God is sovereign and faithful.

Moreover, living out your faith allows you to experience God's promises in real and tangible ways. Acts of obedience and trust often lead to unexpected blessings, such as strengthened relationships, opportunities for growth, and moments of divine provision. Faith becomes a source of resilience, enabling you to endure trials while holding onto hope.

Ultimately, the daily practice of faith is rewarding because it draws you closer to God. As you surrender your plans, seek His guidance, and live according to His Word, you cultivate a relationship with the Creator that is intimate and life-giving. This relationship not only shapes who you are but also equips you to be a light to others, reflecting God's love in everything you do. Though it requires effort, living out your faith each day is an investment in a life filled with meaning, purpose, and eternal significance.

When you give generously, serve humbly, and love selflessly, you bring God's light into a world that desperately needs it. When you resist complacency and stay active in your spiritual walk, you allow God to stretch and grow your faith. And when you cultivate daily habits like journaling, prayer, and obedience, you position yourself to experience His transforming power in every area of your life.

> Faith is not just something you have; it is something you live.

As you step out in faith each day, you'll discover that God is not only transforming your circumstances but also transforming you. Will you choose to live a faith-filled life today?

~❖~

"The God Who Laughs"

> *"The One enthroned in heaven laughs; the Lord scoffs at them."*
> *– Psalm 2:4*

If you think God doesn't have a personality, think again. Just look at the world around us, or better yet, look at yourself. Have you ever stopped to consider the ridiculous situations you find yourself in? You know the ones I'm talking about. Like that time you were tearing the house apart looking for your car keys...only to find them in your hand. Or the time you walked around half the day with mismatched socks and didn't realize it until someone pointed it out.

Let's not forget those moments when you thought the remote control was your cell phone. Or when you poured orange juice into your cereal bowl because you were too tired to focus. And how about that one time you confidently walked into a meeting—only to discover your shirt was on backward?

You can't tell me God isn't sitting on His heavenly throne laughing at our antics. Not out of mockery, but out of love. I imagine Him shaking His head with a grin, saying, "Look at my child. Bless their heart—they're trying."

God's Humor and Our Humanity

Think about it. The Bible says we're made in God's image (Genesis 1:27), and that includes our sense of humor. If we laugh at life's absurdities, wouldn't God, who created laughter, do the same?

Consider Abraham and Sarah. When God told them they'd have a child in their old age, Sarah literally laughed out loud (Genesis 18:12). She thought the idea of having a baby at 90 was so absurd that she couldn't help herself. But guess what? God had the last laugh. When Isaac was born, his name literally meant *laughter*. God turned Sarah's skepticism into a joyful reality.

And let's not overlook Jonah. God told him to preach to Nineveh, but Jonah thought he could outrun God. Really? Who outruns God?

Jonah ended up in the belly of a fish, probably realizing how ridiculous his plan was. I can imagine God giggling, saying, "Oh, Jonah. You really thought that was going to work?"

Faith and Our Foolishness

Here's where it gets serious (sort of). How often do we try to navigate life without tapping into the faith God freely offers us? We stress, panic, and make silly mistakes, all while God's saying, "I've got this, if you'd just trust me."

We pray for guidance but then ignore His answer because it's not what we wanted to hear. We ask for strength but refuse to let go of our burdens. We claim we have faith, yet we act like everything depends on us.

Imagine God watching us like a parent watching a toddler trying to put on shoes. We struggle, get frustrated, and sometimes try to put both feet in one shoe. God's not mad, He's amused because He knows if we'd just ask for help, everything would be fine.

Faith That Makes God Smile

God laughs, but He also loves. He delights in our quirks, our humanity, and even our mistakes because they're opportunities for Him to show us His grace. He's not sitting on His throne shaking His head in disappointment. Instead, He's laughing at our antics and waiting for us to lean on Him.

Take Peter, for example. Peter stepped out of the boat in faith to walk on water toward Jesus (Matthew 14:22-33). But then he saw the wind and waves and started sinking. Can't you just see Jesus reaching out His hand with a knowing smile, saying, "Oh, Peter. Why did you doubt?" It wasn't a rebuke; it was an invitation to trust.

Why God Laughs at Us—and With Us

God doesn't laugh because He's mocking us. He laughs because He loves us. He sees our potential, even when we don't. He knows that our mess-ups aren't the end of the story. In fact, He uses our mistakes to grow our faith.

Faith is God's gift to us, but how often do we forget to unwrap it? He's like, "I gave them this incredible tool to overcome life's challenges, and they're over here using duct tape and wishful thinking instead."

In conclusion, Faith isn't about perfection, it's about progress. It's about trusting God with all the moments, big and small. It's about laughing at ourselves and letting God turn our fumbles into victories.

So, the next time you're running around like a headless chicken or caught in one of life's absurdities, stop and laugh. Then, take a moment to lean into your faith. God's not just watching; He's waiting to help, to guide, and to grow you.

Prayer:

Heavenly Father,

Thank You for the gift of laughter and the reminder that You see us, quirks and all. Help us to trust You in every moment, even when life feels chaotic or absurd. Grow our faith so that we can rely on You more and on ourselves less. Thank You for loving us, for delighting in us, and for turning our fumbles into something beautiful. In Jesus' name, Amen.

"Heaven's authority isn't earned; it's released when faith aligns with God's will and speaks what God has declared."

"Whatever you bind on earth will be bound in heaven, and whatever you loose on earth will be loosed in heaven."
— Matthew 18:18 (NIV)

Chapter 7
PRAYING WITH POWER AND CONFIDENCE

In a world of chaos and uncertainty, one woman's journey from diagnosis to deliverance proves that faith never quits. Witness the power of prayer, the strength of community, and the miracles of a God who is always near. A story that will inspire you to believe again. 'Faith That Transforms: From Tests to Testimonies.

The Transformative Power of Prayer: Activating Faith and Spiritual Authority

In this chapter, we will explore the transformative power of prayer, examining examples from Scripture that illustrate its effectiveness and learning how to pray with confidence, boldness, and faith that moves mountains.

> Prayer is not just a practice; it is an invitation to enter a divine partnership with God.

Through prayer, we don't merely seek Him, we are forever changed by His presence.

Prayer: The Lifeblood of Faith

Faith that transforms is inseparably linked to prayer. Prayer is the sacred channel through which faith is nurtured, activated, and empowered. It is not a ritual or a recitation of words; it is a meeting

place where our hearts align with God's will. In prayer, we are ushered into the holy presence of the Creator, experiencing an intimate relationship that transcends human understanding.

Prayer unites us with the authority of heaven, aligning our desires with God's purposes. Through prayer, we are empowered to overcome spiritual battles, invite the miraculous into our lives, and witness the impossible become possible. Scripture overflows with examples: prayer delivered Daniel from the lion's den, broke chains for Paul and Silas, brought fire from heaven for Elijah, and sustained Jesus as He performed miracles, healed the sick, and raised the dead. Prayer is the engine of spiritual authority, equipping us to conquer fear, overcome sin, and access God's promises of peace, provision, healing, and restoration.

The Barriers to Prayer

Despite its power, prayer is often hindered by barriers that prevent believers from stepping into its transformative potential.

1. Fear and Doubt

Fear of change, fear of the unknown, and even fear of God's blessings can keep us from prayer. Doubts about God's willingness to answer or feelings of unworthiness can paralyze us. The enemy exploits these insecurities, whispering lies that God is distant or indifferent, cutting off our connection to Him and weakening our faith.

2. Distractions and Busyness

In today's fast-paced world, the noise of life can drown out our spiritual hunger. Minds consumed by to-do lists and worldly concerns struggle to focus on God, leaving little room for prayer.

3. Shame and Guilt

Shame over past sins often prevents us from approaching God, even though He already knows our hearts and invites us to come to Him as we are.

These barriers blind us to the magnitude of prayer, a divine invitation to commune with the Creator, who desires to dwell with us, speak to us, and transform us.

Breaking Through: The Limitless Possibilities of Prayer

When we overcome these barriers and step into prayer, the possibilities are limitless. Prayer brings clarity in confusion, courage in fear, strength in weakness, and hope in despair. It opens the floodgates of heaven, releasing blessings, guidance, and peace that surpasses understanding.

Prayer is a sacred space where we invite God's wisdom, power, love, mercy, and holiness into every situation. In this divine exchange, God Himself meets us with His unending grace and fills the gaps in our brokenness. Prayer does more than release God's promises, it recalibrates our relationship with Him. It brings wholeness to our soul.

Prayer as Transformation: How It Changes Us

Through prayer, God gives us Himself, completely and without judgment. It is here that we lay bare our fears and struggles, receiving His peace and strength in return. Prayer is where God reveals His vision for our lives, helping us see ourselves not through the lens of our limitations but through His boundless grace.

As we commune with God in prayer, we are transformed. He renews our minds, reshapes our desires, and equips us to walk in His purpose. Prayer doesn't just change our circumstances, it changes us.

Prayer as Authority: Walking in Victory

Through prayer, God grants us spiritual authority over fear, sin, and the forces of darkness. Jesus declared in Luke 10:19, "I have given you authority to trample on snakes and scorpions and to overcome all the power of the enemy; nothing will harm you." This authority is real, immediate, and available to every believer who prays in faith.

When we pray, we are not pleading with God to act; we are partnering with Him, declaring His will and power over our lives. Prayer shifts our focus from earthly limitations to heavenly possibilities. It empowers us to walk in victory, releasing God's promises and His presence into our circumstances.

The Dynamic Union of Faith and Prayer

Faith and prayer are inseparable. Faith anchors us in the truth of God's promises, while prayer brings those promises into reality. Faith assures us that God is who He says He is; prayer is our response to that belief, calling heaven's realities into earthly situations. Together, they form a powerful partnership that activates God's power and authority in our lives.

When we pray with faith, we step into a transformative relationship with God. He meets us with His love, empowers us with His Spirit, and enables us to bring His glory to earth.

A Call to Pray with Confidence

Prayer that transforms is rooted in confidence, confidence in God's character, His promises, and His ability to do the impossible. Let us step into this sacred partnership with boldness, knowing that when we pray in faith, God's power is unleashed, His presence is revealed, and we are forever changed.

So, pray boldly. Pray faithfully. And watch as your life, and the lives of those around you, are transformed by the power of God.

Prayers of the Righteous: Elijah's Prayer for Rain

The Bible provides countless examples of prayer unlocking God's power and authority, but few are as striking as Elijah's prayer for rain. James 5:16-18 describes the power of a righteous person's prayer:

"The prayer of a righteous person is powerful and effective. Elijah was a human being, even as we are. He prayed earnestly that it would not rain, and it did not rain on the land for three and a half years. Again he prayed, and the heavens gave rain, and the earth produced its crops."

Elijah's prayer wasn't based on his own strength or willpower; it was rooted in faith and alignment with God's purposes. For three and a half years, Elijah's declaration of drought held firm. When the time came for rain, he prayed again, and the heavens opened.

What can we learn from Elijah's example?

1. Boldness: Elijah prayed with confidence, trusting in God's authority.
2. Persistence: Elijah prayed seven times for rain, showing unwavering commitment.
3. Alignment: Elijah's prayer was in harmony with God's will.

Elijah's story reminds us that we, too, can pray with power and effectiveness when we align our prayers with God's purposes.

Aligning with God's Will: Praying with Divine Purpose in Mind

Transformative prayer begins with surrendering our will to God's. Jesus modeled this in the Lord's Prayer, teaching us to say, *"Your kingdom come, Your will be done, on earth as it is in heaven"* (Matthew 6:10).

When we align our prayers with God's will, we unlock His power and authority in our lives. This doesn't mean abandoning our desires, but it does mean trusting that God's plans are higher and better than ours.

Here are key ways to align your prayers with God's will:

1. **Seek God's Word:** The Bible is the foundation of God's revealed will. When we pray according to Scripture, we can pray with confidence. For example, praying for wisdom aligns with James 1:5, which promises that God gives wisdom generously to those who ask.

2. **Listen in Prayer:** Prayer is a two-way conversation. Take time to listen for God's guidance. His Spirit may prompt you to pray in specific ways that align with His purposes.

3. **Surrender Your Agenda:** Faith that transforms trusts God's timing and methods. Be willing to let go of your own plans and trust that He knows what's best.

In conclusion, engaging in prayer as an active demonstration of faith allows individuals to access spiritual authority, thereby influencing their lives and the surrounding environment. Prayer is the doorway to heaven's authority. It is not a passive act but an active expression of faith that transforms our lives and circumstances. When you pray with boldness, persistence, and alignment with God's will, you unlock His power and authority to work in and through you. Like Elijah, you can pray for miracles. Like Jesus, you can surrender your will for a higher purpose. Like Paul, you can pray for transformation that impacts others.

> Faith that transforms doesn't just believe, it speaks, declares, and partners with God in prayer.

The same God who opened the heavens for Elijah, strengthened Jesus in Gethsemane, and empowered Paul's ministry is ready to act in response to your prayers.

From the snowy slopes of West Germany to the depths of your own struggles, this is a story of resilience, faith, and God's unshakable power. Will you rise? Will you trust Him to transform your agony

into victory? This is your moment to embrace the champion's spirit. The next chapter of your life begins now, get ready to soar!

The Thrill of Victory, The Agony of Faith

Life is a journey of peaks and valleys, victories and trials, triumphs and tumbles. But when we fall, whether from failure, heartbreak, or unforeseen setbacks, the true measure of our character is not how flawlessly we live, but how faithfully we rise. As Confucius once said, *"Our greatest glory is not in never falling, but in rising every time we fall."* This is a message of resilience, faith, and the power of God to transform our defeats into triumphs.

This story will inspire you to embrace your challenges, rediscover your faith, and believe in God's ability to restore, redeem, and raise you higher than ever before. With Him, even the most agonizing fall can become the foundation of your greatest victory.

The Agony of Defeat

On March 7, 1970, heavy snow blanketed the slopes at the Ski-Flying World Championships in Oberstdorf, West Germany. Among the competitors was Vinko Bogataj, a young Yugoslavian ski jumper. On his third jump, as snow fell heavily, Vinko lost control and tumbled violently down the slope, crashing into barriers. His fall became infamous as *"the agony of defeat"* on ABC's *Wide World of Sports*.

Though Vinko walked away with minor injuries, his failure was broadcast to millions week after week. The world remembered his fall, but Vinko chose to rise.

Faith Transforms the Fall

Years later, at the 20th anniversary celebration of *Wide World of Sports*, Vinko stood among some of the world's most legendary athletes. Feeling like an outsider, he was surprised when athlete after athlete approached him, not to mock, but to honor him.

"You remind us that failure doesn't define us," one said. Another added, "We all fall. What makes us champions is rising again."

Vinko's story demonstrates that the power to rise comes not from avoiding failure, but from confronting it with resilience and faith. God uses what seems like defeat to build our strength, sharpen our character, and draw us closer to Him.

James 1:2-4 tells us:

"Count it all joy, my brothers, when you meet trials of various kinds, for you know that the testing of your faith produces steadfastness. And let steadfastness have its full effect, that you may be perfect and complete, lacking in nothing."

Trials are not meant to destroy us but to refine us.

They stretch our faith, deepen our trust in God, and prepare us for greater things.

The Victory in Trials

How can we count it joy when life is filled with trials? When we lose a job, face heartbreak, or encounter defeat, how do we find joy? The answer lies in seeing trials not as obstacles but as opportunities for growth.

1. **Trials Produce Strength**: Each fall refines us, teaching us resilience. Like gold purified by fire, we emerge stronger.

2. **Trials Release What's Inside:** Just as a grape must be crushed to release its juice, trials press out the greatness God has placed within us.

3. **Trials Inspire Others:** What looks like defeat to the world can become a testimony of hope for others.

Consider Joseph, betrayed by his brothers and imprisoned in Egypt (Genesis 37–50). What appeared to be a life of setbacks was God's

preparation for a greater purpose. When Joseph rose to power, he not only saved Egypt but also redeemed his family. His story reminds us that *"what others intended for evil, God intended for good"* (Genesis 50:20).

Or think of the apostle Paul, who wrote, *"We rejoice in our sufferings, knowing that suffering produces endurance, and endurance produces character, and character produces hope"* (Romans 5:3-4). Paul's trials, including imprisonment and persecution, became the platform for spreading the Gospel.

Turning Setbacks Into Stepping Stones

God doesn't waste our pain. He turns what the enemy meant for harm into something beautiful. Imagine a seed buried in the dark soil. To the world, it looks dead and forgotten. But beneath the surface, it is transforming, breaking open to release new life.

When we rise from a fall, we show the world that:

➢ Defeat is not final: Falling is not the end—it's the beginning of a comeback.

➢ Faith transforms pain: With God, every setback carries the seed of a greater blessing.

➢ We are never alone: God's hand is always there, lifting us higher than before.

Proverbs 24:16 reminds us: *"The righteous may fall seven times, but they rise again."* Our falls are opportunities to lean on God, to trust His timing, and to see His power at work.

A Champion's Spirit

Vinko's story reminds us of Michael Jordan's famous words: *"I can accept failure; everyone fails at something. But I can't accept not trying."*

God calls us to have the same spirit. When life knocks us down, He whispers, "Get up. I'm not finished with you yet." How amazing is it that God always has more for us to do?

The Gift in Every Fall

As entrepreneur Sara Blakely once said, *"Failure is not the outcome, failure is not trying."* God uses our trials to teach us, shape us, and reveal His greater purpose. What looks like failure to the world is often God's preparation for victory.

Even Jesus faced what seemed like defeat on the cross. Yet, through His resurrection, He turned the ultimate fall into the ultimate victory, bringing salvation to the world.

In conclusion, your greatest glory is not in avoiding failure but in rising every time you fall. With faith, every fall becomes a step toward the victory God has planned for you. Trust Him, and He will give you the courage to rise again and again.

Prayer for Healing, Faith, and Resilience

Heavenly Father,

Thank You for being the God who lifts us up when we fall. In our moments of defeat, remind us that You are not finished with us. Give us the faith to see beyond our failures and trust in Your plans. Restore what is broken in our lives and let us rise with the strength that comes from You.

Lord God, when doubt whispers that we're not enough, fill our hearts with Your promises. Teach us to look for the hidden gifts in every trial and to see adversity as a path to greater blessings.

Thank You for turning our setbacks into stepping stones and our falls into testimonies of Your grace. May we always remember that in You, we are never defeated. We are victorious in Your love.

In Jesus' name, we pray. Amen

"Faith isn't the absence of obstacles; it's the refusal to let them have the final word."

"For everyone born of God overcomes the world. This is the victory that has overcome the world, even our faith." — 1 John 5:4 (NIV)

Chapter 8:
OVERCOMING OBSTACLES TO FAITH

Transformative faith is undeniably powerful, yet it is often tested through challenges that can shake even the most steadfast believer. Why? Because fear, doubt, and unbelief frequently rise up, seeking to erode our trust in God and hinder His power and authority from fully operating in our lives. Where do these challenges stem from? Many times, they are rooted in the lies and schemes of the enemy of darkness, who aims to sow confusion and separation between us and God. However, these obstacles, while formidable, are not insurmountable; rather, they are opportunities for spiritual growth and refinement.

How do we overcome them? It begins by recognizing the enemy's tactics, understanding that these barriers are not from God but designed to draw us away from Him. Once exposed, we can counter them with unwavering faith in God's promises, leaning into His Word as our foundation. Spiritual disciplines such as prayer, worship, fasting, and meditating on Scripture fortify us against the attacks of fear and doubt, grounding us in God's truth and presence. Through these practices, we invite the Holy Spirit to guide and empower us, transforming our struggles into moments of breakthrough.

But what does this breakthrough unlock? Transformative faith unlocks a deeper intimacy with God, enabling us to experience His power, love, and authority in new and profound ways. It grants us access to His supernatural peace in times of chaos, His joy in the midst of trials, and His strength when we feel weak. This faith also

unleashes the promises of healing, provision, and purpose, aligning our lives with God's perfect will. Most importantly, it opens the door to a life marked by spiritual freedom and victory, empowering us to overcome the world's challenges and walk confidently in the identity and calling God has placed on us. Through faith, we become vessels of His transformative power, capable of bringing light into the darkest circumstances and advancing His kingdom on earth.

Recognizing the Enemy's Tactics: Fear as a Spiritual Attack

Fear is one of the enemy's most effective weapons against faith.

It paralyzes, distorts reality, and makes God's promises feel distant. 2 Timothy 1:7 reminds us, *"For God has not given us a spirit of fear, but of power and of love and of a sound mind."*

Fear often disguises itself as rational caution or realistic thinking. It whispers, *"What if God doesn't come through?"* or *"This situation is too big even for God."* But these thoughts are spiritual attacks designed to keep us from stepping into God's power and authority.

The first step to overcoming fear is recognizing it as a tactic of the enemy. When you identify fear, you can choose to replace it with faith. Faith doesn't deny the presence of challenges; it acknowledges them while declaring that God is greater.

Do you not know that the Word of God is our most powerful weapon against doubt and unbelief. When Jesus was tempted in the wilderness, He responded to every attack with Scripture. In the same way, we can counter the enemy's lies with the truth of God's promises.

Here are some key verses to combat unbelief:

1. For fear:

> *"Fear not, for I am with you; be not dismayed, for I am your God. I will strengthen you, yes, I will help you, I will uphold you with My righteous right hand." (Isaiah 41:10)*

2. For doubt:

> *"If you can believe, all things are possible to him who believes." (Mark 9:23)*

3. For uncertainty:

> *"Trust in the Lord with all your heart, and lean not on your own understanding; in all your ways acknowledge Him, and He shall direct your paths." (Proverbs 3:5-6)*

Memorizing and meditating on these promises fortifies your mind and spirit, replacing lies with truth. The more you immerse yourself in God's Word, the more your faith will grow.

Faith Over Feelings: Trusting God When Emotions Don't Align

One of the biggest obstacles to faith is our reliance on emotions. When circumstances are overwhelming, our feelings can make God's promises seem distant or impossible. But faith is not based on feelings; it is rooted deep in God's unchanging character and Word.

Let's consider the story of the disciples in the storm (Matthew 8:23-27). While Jesus slept peacefully, the disciples panicked, allowing their fear to override their faith. They cried out, *"Lord, save us! We're going to drown!"* Jesus rebuked them, saying, *"You of little faith, why are you so afraid?"*

This story reminds us that even when emotions scream danger, we can trust that Jesus is in control. Faith that transforms chooses to believe God's promises, even when feelings of fear or doubt arise.

Practical ways to trust God over feelings include:

➢ Speaking God's promises aloud to remind yourself of His faithfulness.

➢ Worshiping when you feel anxious or fearful, shifting your focus to God.

➢ Seeking wise counsel to gain perspective when emotions cloud your judgment.

Practical Steps: Fasting, Confession, and Spiritual Disciplines

Overcoming obstacles to faith requires intentionality. Faith is strengthened through spiritual disciplines that draw you closer to God and align your heart with His.

1. Fasting:

Fasting is a powerful way to silence the noise of fear and doubt. By denying your physical desires, you create space to focus on God and hear His voice more clearly. Fasting also demonstrates dependence on Him, reinforcing your faith in His provision.

2. Confession:

Doubt and unbelief can take root when left unaddressed. Confessing these struggles to God, and to trusted believers, brings them into the light. James 5:16 encourages us, *"Confess your sins to each other and pray for each other so that you may be healed."* Honesty and accountability are vital for overcoming obstacles to faith.

3. Daily Spiritual Disciplines:

Faith grows through consistent connection with God. Make prayer, Bible study, and worship a regular part of your life. Journaling your prayers and recording answered prayers can also help you track God's faithfulness, building confidence in His power.

Faith Activates God's Promises

> Every promise of God is accessed by faith.

Without it, we cannot receive the blessings He has prepared for us. Romans 4:16 explains, *"Therefore, the promise comes by faith, so that it may be by grace and may be guaranteed to all Abraham's offspring."* This verse points to the relationship between faith, grace, and God's promises. Faith is the channel through which grace flows, allowing us to receive what God has promised.

For example:

➢ Abraham's faith: Abraham believed in God's promise of descendants, even when circumstances (his and Sarah's old age) made it seem impossible. His faith unlocked the fulfillment of God's covenant to make him the father of many nations (Genesis 15:5-6).

Faith is not about earning God's promises but trusting Him enough to receive them. It positions us to experience His supernatural power, even when logic or reality says otherwise. Without faith, God's promises remain inaccessible because faith is what bridges the gap between His will and our circumstances.

Faith Aligns Us with God's Will

Faith is not just about believing God can do something; it's about surrendering our will to His and trusting that His plans are better than ours. James 1:6-7 warns us that doubt disrupts this process: *"But when you ask, you must believe and not doubt, because the one who*

doubts is like a wave of the sea, blown and tossed by the wind. That person should not expect to receive anything from the Lord."

When we walk by faith, we align our hearts with God's purposes rather than insisting on our own plans. This alignment allows His perfect will to be accomplished in our lives. Here are some examples:

➢ Jesus in the Garden of Gethsemane (Luke 22:42): Jesus demonstrated faith when He prayed, *"Father, if you are willing, take this cup from me; yet not my will, but yours be done."* His faith in the Father's plan led to the ultimate sacrifice that brought salvation to humanity.

➢ Noah building the ark (Genesis 6:14-22): Noah obeyed God's instructions to build an ark, even though there was no evidence of a coming flood. His faith in God's warning and plan not only saved his family but also fulfilled God's purpose of preserving humanity and creation.

Faith aligns us with God's will by shifting our perspective from self-reliance to dependence on Him. It helps us see beyond immediate circumstances and trust in His greater plan, even when we don't fully understand it.

Faith Pleases God

Hebrews 11:6 clearly states, *"And without faith it is impossible to please God, because anyone who comes to him must believe that he exists and that he rewards those who earnestly seek him."* This verse highlights two critical components of faith that please God:

1. Believing in His existence, recognizing God as the Creator and Sustainer of all life.

2. Trusting in His character, knowing that He is good, faithful, and able to fulfill His promises.

> Faith pleases God because it demonstrates our complete reliance on Him.

It's not our works, intellect, or resources that move God's heart; it's our trust in who He is and what He can do. Consider these examples:

➤ The centurion's faith (Matthew 8:5-13): When a Roman centurion asked Jesus to heal his servant, he displayed extraordinary faith by saying, *"Just say the word, and my servant will be healed."* Jesus marveled at his faith, saying, *"Truly I tell you, I have not found anyone in Israel with such great faith."* This faith pleased Jesus and led to the servant's healing.

➤ Enoch's life (Hebrews 11:5): Enoch's unwavering faith in God led to his being taken to heaven without experiencing death. His life was marked by a deep relationship with God, which pleased Him greatly.

Faith is necessary to please God because it reflects our trust in His character, His promises, and His purposes. It shows that we acknowledge His sovereignty and depend on Him, not on ourselves.

Faith Empowers Us to Persevere

Faith is what keeps us steady in the face of trials and tribulations. It empowers us to persevere when life feels overwhelming, knowing that God is working behind the scenes for our good. Romans 8:28 reassures us, *"And we know that in all things God works for the good of those who love him, who have been called according to his purpose."*

Examples of perseverance through faith include:

➤ Joseph's journey (Genesis 37-50): Sold into slavery by his brothers, falsely accused, and imprisoned, Joseph never lost faith in God's plan. His faith enabled him to persevere, ultimately leading to his rise as a ruler in Egypt and the fulfillment of God's promise to bless his family.

➤ The Apostle Paul (2 Corinthians 11:23-28): Despite enduring beatings, imprisonment, shipwrecks, and persecution, Paul's

faith kept him focused on his mission to spread the Gospel. He wrote in 2 Corinthians 4:8-9, *"We are hard pressed on every side, but not crushed; perplexed, but not in despair; persecuted, but not abandoned; struck down, but not destroyed."*

Faith gives us the strength to endure because it reminds us that God is faithful, even when circumstances are difficult.

Faith Must Be Attached to Substance to Fulfill God's Purpose:

Faith, in its essence, is not a vague feeling or blind hope. It requires an anchor, something of substance to attach itself to, and that substance is God's Word, His promises, and His character. Without this foundation, faith becomes aimless and ineffective.

Faith Needs Substance

The Bible defines faith in Hebrews 11:1:

> *"Now faith is the substance of things hoped for, the evidence of things not seen."*

Here, "substance" refers to something real, solid, and dependable.

Faith draws its strength from the truth of God's Word.

When faith is attached to the promises and character of God, it has a firm foundation and direction. Without such an anchor, faith would lack the confidence and clarity to accomplish God's purposes.

Faith and the Word of God

Romans 10:17 teaches us:

"So then faith comes by hearing, and hearing by the word of God."

Faith originates and grows when we hear and believe God's Word. His Word is the "substance" that faith clings to, giving it direction

and purpose. For instance, when Peter walked on water in Matthew 14:29, his faith wasn't random, it was attached to Jesus' command, "Come." His faith found substance in Jesus' word, enabling him to step out of the boat. However, when Peter shifted his focus from Jesus to the waves, his faith faltered.

Faith detached from God's purpose becomes wishful thinking or presumption. But when anchored in His will, it fulfills divine plans.

Faith, Action, and Obedience

James 2:17 says, *"Faith by itself, if it does not have works, is dead."* Faith finds expression and fulfillment through action. However, that action must also be grounded in substance. For instance:

➤ The woman with the issue of blood (Mark 5:25-34) believed that touching the hem of Jesus' garment would heal her. Her faith was not random; it was attached to the belief in Jesus' power to heal, and her action confirmed her faith.

➤ Moses lifted his staff at the Red Sea (Exodus 14:16) in obedience to God's command. His faith was attached to God's promise of deliverance.

Faith without a foundation of God's truth leads to inaction or misguided effort. But faith attached to God's Word produces obedience that aligns with His will and fulfills His purposes.

Fear, doubt, and unbelief may try to block your path, but they are no match for the power of God's authority. When you recognize these obstacles as spiritual attacks, counter them with God's Word, and prioritize faith over feelings, you unlock the authority to live victoriously.

Through practical steps like fasting, confession, and spiritual disciplines, you create an environment where faith thrives and transforms every aspect of your life.

> Faith that transforms is not free from challenges, but it is strengthened by overcoming them.

As you persevere, you'll discover that God's power and authority are not only sufficient for your struggles, but they are also transformative, bringing everlasting change to your life and the world around you.

Will you choose today to rise above fear, doubt, and unbelief? God is ready to work through your faith to accomplish the impossible. Step into His promises and experience the life-changing authority of heaven.

In conclusion, overcoming obstacles to faith is a journey that requires intentional effort and reliance on God's strength. By recognizing the enemy's tactics, immersing ourselves in Scripture, trusting God beyond our emotions, and committing to spiritual disciplines, we unlock the transformative power of faith, leading to everlasting change in our lives.

~❖~

Faith on the Fast Track

Imagine a young girl, frail and broken, her body a prisoner of illness and her dreams dismissed as impossible. Doctors told her she would never walk again, let alone run. But she refused to believe them. Instead, she believed in something greater, a faith that unlocked the power of trusting in God's purpose for her life. That faith didn't just carry her, it transformed her. This is the story of Wilma Rudolph, a living testimony that faith can change your destiny for the better.

You may not know Wilma Rudolph. She was born long before many of us were even a thought in our parents' minds, but her story is timeless. She is a legend, a beacon of hope for anyone facing impossible odds. Her life shouts a message that resonates across generations: *You too are Wilma Rudolph.* You too are destined to exceed against all odds. You too have a purpose that no one can deny.

Faith isn't just hope, it's the ability to trust in God's higher plan, even when circumstances seem bleak. When the doctors told Wilma Rudolph's mother that her daughter would never walk again, Blanche

Rudolph turned to faith. She didn't just accept the prognosis; she sought God's purpose in her daughter's life and believed He had a greater destiny for her.

Wilma inherited that same faith. She would not allow herself to believe the doctor's words. Faith became her anchor, unlocking the determination she needed to endure grueling therapy and push past every obstacle. With every brace she wore and every painful step she took, Wilma's faith deepened her trust in God's plan. She came to believe that her life had a purpose far greater than her limitations.

Faith gives us a divine perspective.

> It allows us to see beyond the immediate struggle to the future glory God has prepared.

For Wilma, faith not only allowed her to walk again but to run—to break records, shatter barriers, and inspire generations. Faith changed her destiny for the better, aligning her with God's plan and giving her the courage to take the steps that would define her life.

Wilma's refusal to accept the doctor's prognosis was an act of faith. While science and medicine told her one thing, her faith in God told her another. This kind of faith doesn't deny reality but acknowledges that God's power transcends it. Her mother reminded her daily, "God has a plan for you," and that belief became the foundation of Wilma's resilience.

At six years old, Wilma was told she would never walk again. Yet by twelve, she was not only walking but running. What made the difference? Faith. It was her belief that God's purpose for her life was bigger than any disability. She aligned her determination with that belief, and it transformed her.

Faith teaches us that limitations are not the end of the story; they are the beginning of God's work in our lives. When Wilma rejected the limitations imposed on her by doctors, she chose instead to believe in a future she could not yet see, a future filled with strength, victory, and purpose.

You may not face the same challenges Wilma faced, but like her, you are destined for greatness. God has placed a purpose in your life, and nothing, no sickness, no failure, no opinion of others, can take it away.

When Wilma Rudolph ran, she wasn't just running for medals; she was running for everyone who had ever been told, *You can't.* She was running for the people who were denied opportunities because of their race, their gender, or their circumstances. She ran to prove that God's purpose cannot be thwarted, no matter what obstacles stand in the way.

And just like Wilma, you are destined to run your own race. Maybe you've been told that you're not smart enough, strong enough, or capable enough. Maybe the world has tried to deny you of what God has for you. But let Wilma's story remind you: the world doesn't have the final say. God does.

When you trust in Him, He will guide you past every hurdle, over every setback, and through every trial. You too are Wilma Rudolph. You too can exceed against all odds.

Wilma Rudolph's life is a prime example of how faith can rewrite your destiny. Born into limitless means and plagued by illness, her early life seemed destined for hardship. But her faith in God and her belief in His plan opened doors she could have never imagined.

Faith doesn't just change your circumstances; it transforms you. It gives you the courage to move forward when the odds are stacked against you. It aligns your steps with God's will, setting you on a path that leads to a better future. For Wilma, faith not only helped her to overcome polio but also carried her to the pinnacle of athletic achievement, where she became an Olympic champion.

This is the power of faith: it unlocks the strength, courage, and determination needed to fulfill God's purpose. It redefines what is possible, reminding us that with God, all things are possible (Matthew 19:26).

Faith in Action: Determination Fueled by God's Purpose

Faith ignited Wilma's determination, but it was her alignment with God's purpose that gave her story its power. Her relentless drive to overcome polio and pursue athletics wasn't just about personal ambition—it was about glorifying God. By trusting in His plan, she became a vessel of His power, showing the world what faith can achieve.

In conclusion, Wilma Rudolph's story is a living testimony of the power of faith. It shows us that trusting in God's purpose not only transforms our lives but also allows us to become vessels of His glory. From a little girl who was told she'd never walk again to an Olympic champion; Wilma's life reminds us that faith can change our destiny.

When faith aligns you with God's purpose, it unlocks a power greater than your circumstances. Trust in Him, take the steps He's calling you to take, and let Him transform your life. You too are Wilma Rudolph. Run your race with faith, and claim what God has for you.

Prayer:

Heavenly Father,

We come before You in awe of Your power, Your purpose, and the way You weave every trial into triumph for those who trust in You. Lord, just as You carried Wilma Rudolph through her struggles, we ask that You strengthen us today. Let the same faith that unlocked her destiny ignite in us the courage to believe in Your promises and to walk boldly into the plans You have for our lives.

Father, we know that Your Word declares, *"For I know the plans I have for you, plans to prosper you and not to harm you, plans to give you a hope and a future"* (Jeremiah 29:11). We hold fast to that promise, trusting that no sickness, no failure, no rejection, and no setback can separate us from Your love and purpose.

We declare that no weapon formed against us will prosper (Isaiah 54:17). No word of doubt, no circumstance, no obstacle will have the final say over our lives. Only Your Word, spoken before the foundation of the world, will come to pass.

Finally, Lord, we pray for others who are struggling, those who feel defeated, forgotten, or disqualified. Use us to be a light to them, as You used Wilma's life to inspire and transform countless others. May our stories of faith, perseverance, and victory glorify You and draw others closer to Your heart.

In the mighty name of Jesus, who makes all things possible, we pray.

Amen.

"Faith is heaven's access point, where the natural ends and the supernatural begins."

"His divine power has given us everything we need for a godly life through our knowledge of him."
— 2 Peter 1:3 (NIV)

Chapter 9:

ACCESSING DIVINE POWER THROUGH FAITH

Transformative faith does not originate from mere human effort or sheer willpower; rather, it is a divine work ignited and sustained by the power of the Holy Spirit. It is not something we manufacture through discipline or determination alone, but a supernatural gift that reshapes our hearts, renews our minds, and empowers us to live in alignment with God's will. This kind of faith moves beyond intellectual belief, it penetrates the soul, producing a deep and abiding trust in God that manifests in a life of obedience, love, and spiritual strength.

Why? Because without the Spirit's divine guidance, believers remain limited by their own understanding and strength, unable to fully access the boundless power and authority of God that brings true, lasting transformation. The Spirit is the bridge between our human frailty and God's infinite resources, making the impossible possible in our lives.

Why is this so essential? Walking in the Spirit is not a passive experience but an active, daily partnership, a communion that continually shapes our hearts and renews our minds. It is through this relationship that we are empowered to live in unwavering faith, manifest the fruit of the Spirit, and step into the supernatural realm of God's gifts and purposes. The Holy Spirit equips us to move beyond superficial change, enabling us to embrace the fullness of God's will and live as living vessels of His transformative power.

This chapter explores the role of the Holy Spirit in faith, the transformative power of His fruits and gifts, and practical steps to stay connected to His leading.

Who is the Holy Spirit? Understanding His Role in Faith

> The Holy Spirit is God's presence within us, sent to guide, empower, and sustain our faith.

Jesus promised the Spirit as our Helper in John 14:26, saying, *"But the Helper, the Holy Spirit, whom the Father will send in My name, will teach you all things and bring to your remembrance all that I have said to you."*

The Spirit's role is multifaceted. He:

➢ Teaches us God's truth (John 16:13).

➢ Convicts us of sin and leads us to repentance (John 16:8).

➢ Empowers us to live in God's will (Acts 1:8).

➢ Intercedes for us in prayer (Romans 8:26-27).

Faith that transforms begins with acknowledging the Spirit's active presence and inviting Him to take the lead in every aspect of life.

The Fruits and Gifts of the Spirit: How They Work Through Believers

The transformative work of the Holy Spirit is evident in two ways: through the fruits of the Spirit and the gifts of the Spirit.

1. The Fruits of the Spirit:

The fruits of the Spirit, described in Galatians 5:22-23, are the evidence of a life surrendered to God: *"Love, joy, peace, patience, kindness, goodness, faithfulness, gentleness, and self-control."*

These fruits transform our character, allowing us to reflect Christ in our relationships and actions. For example, faithfulness grows our trust in God, while peace helps us remain steady in difficult circumstances.

2. The Gifts of the Spirit:

The Spirit also equips believers with supernatural gifts to build up the church and advance God's kingdom. These gifts, outlined in 1 Corinthians 12:8-10, include wisdom, knowledge, faith, healing, miracles, prophecy, and discernment.

The gifts of the Spirit are not earned; they are given by God for His glory. Faith unlocks these gifts, allowing the Spirit to work through us in ways that surpass human ability.

Faith's Dependence on the Spirit: Staying Connected to His Guidance

Walking in the Spirit requires an ongoing relationship with Him. Faith depends on this connection, as it is the Spirit who sustains and strengthens our trust in God. Romans 8:14 reminds us, *"For those who are led by the Spirit of God are the children of God."*

To walk in the Spirit, we must:

1. **Stay spiritually alert:** The Spirit speaks in a still, small voice. Regular prayer and time in God's Word keep us attuned to His guidance.
2. **Yield control:** Walking in the Spirit means surrendering our plans and trusting Him to direct our steps.
3. **Obey promptly:** When the Spirit prompts us to act, delayed obedience is disobedience. Faith responds immediately, trusting that God knows best.

In conclusion, Faith that transforms is a journey of walking in the Spirit. The Holy Spirit empowers us to live beyond human limita-

tions, unlocking God's power and authority in ways that bring everlasting change.

By bearing the fruits of the Spirit, exercising His gifts, and staying connected to His guidance, you can experience a life of supernatural faith. The same Spirit who raised Christ from the dead dwells in you, ready to lead, equip, and empower you for every step of your journey.

~❖~

"When the winds rage and the waves crash, how do you hold on? What if the key to peace isn't found in the absence of the storm but in the One who can calm it?"

Faith in the Storm

Life can change in an instant. One moment, you're walking under the warmth of a clear sky, and the next, a storm crashes in, leaving you disoriented, scared, and grasping for answers. The storms of life, whether they are financial struggles, health crises, relationship turmoil, or unexpected grief, can feel overwhelming.

But there's good news: while storms are inevitable, fear doesn't have to define your story. Through faith, we unlock God's transforming power, experiencing His authority over even the most violent winds and waves. The same Jesus who calmed the Sea of Galilee can bring peace to the storms in your life.

The Storm, the Savior, and the Faith That Transforms

The sun was setting over the Sea of Galilee as Jesus and His disciples climbed into the boat. Exhausted from ministering to the crowds, Jesus lay down in the stern, His head resting on a cushion. The disciples rowed, enjoying the tranquil waters. But as the night deepened, dark clouds gathered on the horizon, and the sea turned restless.

Without warning, a violent storm erupted. The waves surged, crashing against the boat and spilling icy water over its sides. The dis-

ciples, seasoned fishermen, fought to keep the vessel afloat. Fear clawed at their hearts.

"Wake Him up!" Peter shouted over the roar of the wind. "Doesn't He care that we're about to drown?"

Jesus woke to their cries, stood, and stretched out His hand. "Peace, be still!" He commanded.

In an instant, the wind stopped, and the sea became as calm as glass. The disciples stared at Him in awe. "Who is this man?" they whispered. "Even the wind and the waves obey Him."

Though the storm terrified the disciples, Jesus used it to teach them a profound lesson: faith in Him is greater than fear. They learned that Jesus has authority over everything, nature, circumstances, and even the chaos of life.

We can face our storms with faith. Like the disciples, we often panic when life's storms hit, forgetting the power of the One who is in the boat with us. Whether you're facing a sudden job loss, a devastating diagnosis, or the breakdown of a relationship, the key to overcoming the storm is faith in God's unchanging promises.

1. Acknowledge the Storm, but Trust the Savior

When the storm hits, it's natural to feel fear. But don't let it consume you. Acknowledge the reality of your situation, then remind yourself of who Jesus is the One who calms storms, heals the brokenhearted, and makes a way where there seems to be none.

When Amelia lost her job unexpectedly, fear overwhelmed her. Bills were piling up, and she didn't know how she'd provide for her children. But instead of letting fear paralyze her, Amelia prayed daily, asking God for wisdom and provision. She trusted Him to guide her next steps, and within weeks, she found a new job, one that paid more and allowed her more time with her kids.

2. Speak God's Promises Over Your Life

In the midst of the storm, declare the promises of Scripture. Speak words of life, not despair. God's Word reminds us:

> ➤ *"Be still and know that I am God"* (Psalm 46:10).

> ➤ *"Do not fear, for I am with you"* (Isaiah 41:10).

> ➤ *"The Lord will fight for you; you need only to be still"* (Exodus 14:14).

When Tim received a cancer diagnosis, he was terrified. But instead of succumbing to fear, he clung to Psalm 23:4: *"Even though I walk through the darkest valley, I will fear no evil, for You are with me."* During his treatment, Tim shared his faith and personal testimony with others at the hospital, serving as a source of inspiration to both patients and staff.

3. Lean Into Prayer and Community

Storms are easier to face when we invite God into the boat and surround ourselves with people who encourage and pray for us. Faith flourishes in community.

After Olivia's husband passed away suddenly, she joined a grief support group at her church. She found strength through prayer and the support of others who had walked similar roads. As her faith deepened, she began ministering to others, turning her pain into purpose.

In conclusion, when Jesus calmed the storm, He not only demonstrated His power over nature but also His deep care for His disciples. That same Jesus cares for you. Whatever storm you're facing today, remember: He is in the boat with you, and His authority is greater than any wind or wave.

Storms may be unavoidable, but fear is not. When life changes in an instant, let your faith anchor you.

Jesus never promised a life without storms, but He did promise His presence. And in His presence, there is peace, power, and transformation.

A Prayer for Faith in the Storm

Heavenly Father,

Thank You for being our anchor in life's storms. When fear rises and the waves crash around us, remind us of Your unchanging love and power. Help us to trust You, even when we can't see the outcome, knowing that You are always working for our good. Strengthen our faith so that we may walk in peace, no matter the storm. In Jesus' name, Amen.

Remember: Faith transforms fear. With Jesus in your boat, you are never alone, and the storm is never the end of your story.

"Restoration begins when faith stops rehearsing the ruins and starts declaring God's rebuilding power."

"I will restore to you the years that the swarming locust has eaten." — Joel 2:25 (NKJV)

Chapter 10:
FAITH THAT HEALS

Faith that transforms goes beyond mere spiritual growth; it encompasses restoration, addressing the brokenness in every facet of our lives and showcasing God's unparalleled power and authority. This transformative faith reveals itself through healing, whether from physical ailments, emotional wounds, or spiritual struggles. The promise of healing is a recurring theme throughout Scripture, a testament to God's unwavering desire to make us whole.

But how does this healing come to life? Faith serves as the critical key, unlocking the depth of God's restorative power. It opens the door to divine intervention, enabling us to experience His presence and promises fully. Through faith, we are invited to trust in His timing, lean on His sovereignty, and witness His ability to heal, redeem, and restore every area of our lives. In this way, faith not only strengthens our spiritual walk but also manifests God's transformative power in tangible, life-changing ways.

The healing ministry of Jesus reveals God's heart for restoration. Throughout the Gospels, Jesus repeatedly demonstrated His power and authority to heal, meeting people in their suffering and restoring them to wholeness.

Consider Matthew 8:16-17, which says, *"When evening came, many who were demon-possessed were brought to him, and he drove out the spirits with a word and healed all the sick. This was to fulfill what was spoken through the prophet Isaiah: 'He took up our infirmities and bore our diseases.'"*

Healing was not a side activity in Jesus' ministry, it was central to His mission of bringing the kingdom of God to earth. Each miracle of healing was a glimpse of God's ultimate plan to restore all creation.

Faith that heals begins with understanding that God desires restoration for His people. He is not distant or indifferent to our pain but actively works to redeem it.

One of the most profound stories of healing in the Bible is that of the woman with the issue of blood. For twelve years, she had suffered physically and emotionally, exhausting her resources in search of a cure. Yet her faith led her to Jesus.

We see in Mark 5:28 her thought process, "If I just touch his clothes, I will be healed." Despite the crowd pressing around Jesus, she reached out in faith and touched His garment. Immediately, she was healed. Jesus, sensing power had gone out from Him, turned and said, *"Daughter, your faith has healed you. Go in peace and be freed from your suffering."*

This story illustrates the transformative power of faith. The woman's healing was not just physical, it restored her dignity, identity, and relationship with God. Her faith activated Jesus' power, breaking through barriers of fear and doubt to receive His promise of restoration.

Faith that heals is not limited to the miraculous events of the Bible; it is available to believers today. Here are practical steps to pray for and experience healing:

1. Believe in God's Power and Willingness to Heal:

Healing begins with faith in God's ability and desire to restore. Pray with the confidence that He hears you and wants to work in your life.

2. Speak the Word of God Over Your Situation:

Scripture is filled with promises of healing. Declare verses like Isaiah 53:5, *"By His wounds we are healed,"* and Jeremiah 30:17, *"I will*

restore you to health and heal your wounds." Speaking these promises strengthens your faith and aligns your prayers with God's will.

3. Invite Others to Pray with You:

There is power in agreement. James 5:14-15 encourages believers to pray for one another, saying, *"The prayer of faith will save the sick, and the Lord will raise him up."* Surrounding yourself with faith-filled believers can bolster your trust in God's healing power.

4. Trust God's Timing and Process:

Sometimes healing is instantaneous, and other times it unfolds over weeks, months, or years. Trust that God's timing is perfect and that His plan for you is good.

Testimonies of healing remind us that God's power and authority are alive and active today. Consider these testimonies:

➤ A woman diagnosed with terminal cancer was prayed over by her church. Despite the doctors' prognosis, her faith and the prayers of others brought complete healing. Her scans showed no trace of cancer, and she now testifies of God's power to everyone he meets.

➤ A woman struggling with severe depression experienced emotional healing through a small group's prayers. Over time, God restored her joy and peace, allowing her to minister to others walking through similar struggles.

➤ A family facing financial hardship prayed for God's intervention. Though their need was material, their prayers for restoration were answered as God provided opportunities, resources, and emotional healing from the stress they endured.

These stories reflect the truth that faith transforms and restores in every area of life, physically, emotionally, and spiritual.

In conclusion, Faith that heals is faith that transforms. It recognizes God's power and authority and invites His promise of restoration into every area of life. Whether you are seeking healing for yourself

or standing in the gap for someone else, trust that God is still in the business of miracles.

As you step out in faith, remember the words of Jesus in John 14:12: *"Very truly I tell you, whoever believes in me will do the works I have been doing, and they will do even greater things than these."*

Healing is not just a possibility; it is a promise. Allow your faith to activate God's power, and watch as He brings restoration, unlocking His authority for everlasting change. Will you reach out in faith like the woman with the issue of blood? Your healing could be just a touch away.

Consider this:

1. **God's Will to Heal:** Healing is central to God's mission of restoration, as demonstrated through Jesus' ministry. His miracles reflect His desire to heal physical, emotional, and spiritual brokenness.

2. **Faith Activates Healing**: The woman with the issue of blood illustrates how faith breaks through barriers to access God's restorative power. Her healing was not just physical but holistic, restoring her dignity and relationship with God.

3. **Practical Steps for Healing:**

   * Believe in God's power and willingness to heal.

   * Declare Scripture over your situation to align your faith with God's promises.

   * Seek prayer from a community of believers for added support.

   * Trust in God's timing and process, knowing His plans are good.

4. **Testimonies Inspire Faith**: Today's stories of healing remind us that God's power is active today, bringing restoration in physical health, emotional well-being, and life circumstances.

Our final thought is Faith that heals is faith that restores. When we trust God's power and promises, we invite Him to transform our brokenness into a testimony of His love and authority. His healing isn't just for the past, it's for today and for all who believe.

~❖~

Overcoming Doubt and Trusting God's Direction

There are moments in life when we feel incapable of doing what seems impossible. We second-guess ourselves, even when we know that it is God who is directing us.

> Have you ever had a moment where you knew God was speaking to you, guiding you toward a specific path, but you still hesitated?

Have you ever questioned whether it was truly His voice?

You might ask, "God, is this really You?" or "Is this the right path for my life?" Maybe you've prayed, "Lord, should I take this job?" "Should I enter into this relationship?" or "Is this opportunity aligned with Your will?" Yet, despite hearing His guidance, doubt creeps in, making you second-guess His direction.

Why do we do this? Why do we struggle to fully trust God, even after asking Him for clarity? The answer lies in our human nature, we rely too much on what we see, feel, and understand, rather than walking by faith. The Bible tells us in Proverbs 3:5-6:

"Trust in the Lord with all your heart, and lean not on your own understanding; in all your ways submit to him, and he will make your paths straight."

Faith is what gives us clarity. It aligns us with God's will and allows us to perceive His desires in any given situation. Without faith, we rely solely on human reasoning, which is limited and flawed. But faith takes us beyond what we can see, into the realm of the supernatural.

Faith is not just about believing that God can do something; it is trusting that He will do what He has promised. The Bible tells us in Hebrews 11:1: "Now faith is the substance of things hoped for, the evidence of things not seen." When we must make a decision, faith ushers us into the presence of God. It silences fear and uncertainty, reminding us that God is in control. Faith allows us to step forward, even when we don't have all the answers.

Confidence in the Creator of the Universe

When you trust God in your situation you now have confidence in the Creator of the Universe. You are really showing God that you have confidence in Him. Can you imagine not having confidence in the One who created the universe with just His spoken word?

Genesis 1 records that God spoke the world into existence:

"And God said, 'Let there be light,' and there was light." (Genesis 1:3)

If He could create the heavens and the earth just by speaking, how much more can He handle the details of your life?

To doubt God's direction is to doubt His ability to guide and sustain you. It is similar to when my children were young and hesitated to jump into their father's arms for an airplane ride, despite knowing that their father had never dropped them before. God is faithful, and He never fails. Faith tells us that no matter what is in front of us, it cannot compare to what is behind us. What does that mean? It means that the Word of God, the foundation of our faith, has always been there. It sustains us, strengthens us, upholds us, and directs us.

Jesus Himself illustrated the power of God's Word when He resisted the devil's temptations in the wilderness. Each time Satan tried to deceive Him, Jesus responded with Scripture, saying, "It is written..." (Matthew 4:4, 7, 10). This teaches us that the Word of God is our foundation in times of doubt and decision-making.

When we second-guess God's direction, we must return to His Word. Isaiah 55:11 reassures us:

"So is my word that goes out from my mouth: It will not return to me empty, but will accomplish what I desire and achieve the purpose for which I sent it." If God has spoken a promise over your life, it will come to pass. Your job is to trust Him, even when you don't see how it will happen.

Faith transforms us by shifting our focus from our insufficiencies to God's sufficiency. Our human thoughts, fears, and limitations are exchanged for the supernatural power of God. But why would God want to do that for us?

One reason is simple: He loves us. But more importantly, God always keeps His word. Numbers 23:19 says: "God is not a man, that He should lie, nor a son of man, that He should change His mind. Does He speak and then not act? Does He promise and not fulfill?"

Faith Is Like Money in the Bank

Think of faith as spiritual currency. Just as money is backed by gold, faith is backed by the integrity of God's Word. If you are holding a check issued by a reputable source, you may still feel some reluctance to cash it. You believe that the funds are there.

Likewise, when God gives you a promise, it is backed by His authority. 2 Corinthians 1:20 declares: "For all the promises of God in Him are Yes, and in Him Amen, to the glory of God through us."

When we hesitate to trust God, it is like holding a check from a billionaire and questioning whether the money is real. But the Bible reminds us that: "For every beast of the forest is Mine, the cattle on a thousand hills." (Psalm 50:10)

This verse emphasizes that God owns everything. He is sovereign over all creation, and His resources are unlimited. So why do we doubt? If God owns it all, then His provision is endless.

Faith in God is a continuous move of His authority, He remains God, and His promises never end.

Let's look at some biblical examples of Faith vs. Doubt

1. Peter Walking on Water – Matthew 14:28-31

Peter walked on water when Jesus called him, but the moment he took his eyes off Jesus and focused on the storm, he sank. Why? Because doubt crept in. This shows us that faith requires focus, keeping our eyes on Jesus, not our circumstances.

2. The Israelites Doubting God's Provision – Numbers 13:30-33

When God promised the Israelites the land of Canaan, Moses sent spies to scout the land. Ten spies came back fearful, saying the land was full of giants. Only Joshua and Caleb had faith, believing God would fulfill His promise. The Israelites' doubt caused them to wander the wilderness for 40 years instead of entering the Promised Land immediately.

This example reminds us that doubt delays our destiny. Faith moves us forward; doubt keeps us stuck.

Final Encouragement: Walk by Faith, Not by Sight

God is always speaking, always guiding, always providing. But will you trust Him? Will you stop second-guessing His voice?

Faith is not about having all the answers; it's about trusting the One who does, because He knows your future.

When doubt tries to creep in, remind yourself:

➤ God's Word never fails.

➤ His promises are secure.

➤ He owns the cattle on a thousand hills, His resources are endless.

So step forward in faith. Trust Him. He has already gone before you.

Faith in the Midst of Uncertainty: Carol's Story

Carol gripped the steering wheel, her knuckles turning colors as she stared out at the rain streaking across her windshield. The news she had just received felt like a gut punch, her company was relocating out of town, and she had two choices: move to another state or lose her job.

Why now, God? she thought, shaking her head.

Things were finally starting to come together. After years of struggling, after enduring a painful divorce that had shattered her confidence, she had just started rebuilding. She had bought a new home, her kids were thriving in their new school, and for the first time in a long time, she had peace. And now this?

Tears welled up in her eyes as she whispered, "Lord, what am I supposed to do?"

Her mind raced with a thousand questions. If she moved, she would have to uproot her children again. If she stayed, she had no idea how she would pay the mortgage. The fear of the unknown loomed over her like a storm cloud.

Then, in the quiet of the car, she heard a familiar voice, not an audible voice, but the echo of wisdom that had been planted in her heart long ago. It was her mother's voice:

"Baby, God won't put more on you than you can bear."

She exhaled sharply, closing her eyes. Those words had carried her through so many dark moments in her life, and they reminded her of 1 Corinthians 10:13:

"No temptation has overtaken you except what is common to mankind. And God is faithful; he will not let you be tempted beyond what you can bear. But when you are tempted, he will also provide a way out so that you can endure it."

Carol straightened in her seat. God is still in control. He's never left me before, and He's not about to start now.

With renewed determination, she wiped away her tears and spoke out loud, "Lord, my faith tells me that You are still in control, and I'm not about to throw in the towel."

When God Closes One Door, He Opens Another

Later that night, Carol sat at her kitchen table, mindlessly scrolling through Facebook, still wrestling with what to do next. Then, ping!, a notification popped up.

It was a message from an old friend.

Hey Carol! I don't know if you're looking, but there's an opening at my job. It pays more, has better benefits, and you wouldn't have to move.

Her heart pounded as she read the message again. Could this be it? Could this be the answer she had been praying for?

Carol immediately thought of Ephesians 3:20:

"Now to him who is able to do immeasurably more than all we ask or imagine, according to his power that is at work within us."

She laughed out loud, shaking her head. God, You're something else.

At that moment, she realized something powerful: faith isn't just believing when things are easy, it's holding on when everything seems to be falling apart.

God's Promises Are Secure. You Can Bank on It

As she sat at the kitchen table, sipping her coffee, Carol reflected on how faithful God had been. When she thought she had hit rock bottom, He had made a way. And not just any way, He had provided something better than what she had before.

She thought about how, just hours ago, she had been sitting in her car, feeling like her world was collapsing. But God had already gone before her, setting things in motion.

She smiled, remembering the words of 2 Corinthians 1:20:

"For all the promises of God in Him are Yes, and in Him Amen, to the glory of God through us."

When God says something, you can absolutely bank on it.

Just like money in the bank is backed by something of value, God's promises are backed by His power, His authority, and His unchanging nature. She thought of Psalm 50:10: "For every beast of the forest is mine, and the cattle upon a thousand hills."

God owns it all. His provision is endless, and His timing is perfect.

Carol had almost let fear make her doubt Him. But she realized that God had already written the next chapter before she even knew the page was turning.

Faith: Trusting the One Who Knows the Future

Carol was uncertain about what the future might bring, but she had confidence in the One who did. And that was enough.

God is the Alpha and the Omega, the Beginning and the End (Revelation 22:13). He sees what we cannot see. He knows the outcome before we even face the problem. And faith reminds us that God knows our situation better than we do.

She took a deep breath and whispered, "Lord, I trust You."

And just like that, peace filled her heart. She didn't have all the answers, but she had God. And that was more than enough.

Final Encouragement: Trust the God Who Never Fails

Maybe you're like Carol—facing a situation that seems impossible. Maybe you're second-guessing God's direction. But let Carol's story remind you:

➢ God never abandons His children.

- ➢ He already has the next step prepared for you.
- ➢ His promises never fail.

Faith in God is a continuous move of His authority. He is God, and His promises never end.

So, whatever you're facing today, hold on. Keep trusting. Because when God says something, you can absolutely bank on it.

"You weren't created to merely survive, you were anointed to rule. Faith activates the dominion already written in your design."

"Let them have dominion... over all the earth."
— Genesis 1:26 (KJV)

Chapter 11

OPERATING IN THE DOMINION GIVEN TO YOU

Faith that transforms is not merely for personal growth or comfort. It is an active force designed to unlock God's power and authority in believers' lives, equipping them to impact the world for His glory. True faith connects us to God's greater mission, a purpose far beyond ourselves. It transforms our lives and empowers us to bring His love, truth, and authority into every corner of the earth.

Faith is not a passive feeling; it is a dynamic force that moves us toward action. The transformative power of faith begins within but radiates outward, touching the lives of those around us.

> ➢ "You are the light of the world. A town built on a hill cannot be hidden" (Matthew 5:14).

> ➢ "In the same way, let your light shine before others, that they may see your good deeds and glorify your Father in heaven" (Matthew 5:16).

Faith compels us to step into God's plans and purposes, empowering us to extend His love and truth to the world. As vessels of His power, believers are equipped to fulfill His mission, shining as lights in a world desperate for hope.

The question every believer must answer is: How are we impacting the world for Christ? God's purpose for our lives transcends personal ambitions. We are intricately woven into His Kingdom work, called to align our lives with His divine mission.

➤ "For we are God's handiwork, created in Christ Jesus to do good works, which God prepared in advance for us to do" (Ephesians 2:10).

➤ "Go into all the world and preach the gospel to all creation" (Mark 16:15).

As ambassadors of Christ, our role is to reflect His love and truth to the world. This requires a faith that is alive and active, one that demonstrates God's power through tangible actions.

➤ "We are therefore Christ's ambassadors, as though God were making his appeal through us" (2 Corinthians 5:20).

Faith Unlocks God's Power and Authority

Walking in faith aligns us with God's authority, enabling Him to work through us. Faith is the key to accessing divine resources and accomplishing what would otherwise be impossible.

➤ "Very truly I tell you, whoever believes in me will do the works I have been doing, and they will do even greater things than these, because I am going to the Father" (John 14:12).

➤ "Now to him who is able to do immeasurably more than all we ask or imagine, according to his power that is at work within us" (Ephesians 3:20).

Faith emboldens us to take risks for God's glory, to act boldly, and to trust Him to bring about transformation.

> Faith is not just for our comfort; it is a call to action.

Our lives should point others to Christ through our words, deeds, and unwavering commitment to Him.

➤ "You did not choose me, but I chose you and appointed you so that you might go and bear fruit, fruit that will last" (John 15:16).

➤ "By this everyone will know that you are my disciples, if you love one another" (John 13:35).

Every step of obedience, every act of faith, and every moment of love has the potential to impact eternity.

God created humanity to operate in dominion, His authority to steward, govern, and influence creation according to His will. Genesis 1:28 declares:

"Be fruitful and increase in number; fill the earth and subdue it. Rule over the fish in the sea and the birds in the sky and over every living creature that moves on the ground."

This divine mandate reveals God's intent for humanity: to govern creation under His authority. Sin disrupted this purpose, leaving humanity powerless. However, through Christ, believers are restored to their position of authority, no longer victims of circumstances but victors in His Kingdom.

Dominion is not about self-serving control but about partnering with God to fulfill His will on earth.

Jesus reintroduced the concept of kingdom authority during His ministry, empowering His followers to operate with divine power. "I have given you authority to trample on snakes and scorpions and to overcome all the power of the enemy; nothing will harm you" (Luke 10:19).

This authority is not based on personal merit but on our identity in Christ. As ambassadors of God's Kingdom, we carry His authority to represent Him and enforce His will on earth.

1. **Authority over the enemy:** Through Christ, we have power to resist the devil and command him to flee (James 4:7).

2. **Authority in prayer:** Jesus promised in John 14:13, "And I will do whatever you ask in my name, so that the Father may be glorified in the Son." Praying in Jesus' name is exercising kingdom authority.

3. **Authority to speak life:** Proverbs 18:21 reminds us that life and death are in the power of the tongue. Believers are called to de-

clare God's will over situations, releasing His power into their lives.

By walking in kingdom authority, we bring heaven's solutions to earthly problems, transforming lives and circumstances through God's power. Kingdom authority is not a vague concept—it is meant to be lived out daily. Faith that transforms empowers believers to take dominion in specific areas:

1. **Family:** Speak life and blessings over your household. Pray for peace, unity, and restoration in your relationships, trusting God to intervene in difficult situations.

2. **Workplace:** Bring God's principles into your job. Pray for wisdom and favor, and declare His solutions over challenges in your work environment.

3. **Ministry:** Step into your calling with confidence, sharing the gospel, praying for the sick, and trusting God to manifest His power through you.

Walking in dominion means aligning every area of your life with God's will, allowing His authority to flow through you for God's glory.

In conclusion, faith that transforms unlocks the power and authority God has given believers to operate in His Kingdom. You are not powerless, you are called to bring His dominion into every aspect of life, reflecting His glory and advancing His purposes. This authority is not about human strength but about God's power working through your faith. When you speak His Word, declare His promises, and trust His will, you activate heaven's transformative power on earth.

God's authority is already within you. Step into it boldly, and watch Him use you to bring lasting change to your family, workplace, and ministry.

Prayer for Empowerment and Transformation

Heavenly Father,

Thank You for calling us to a mission greater than ourselves. We humbly acknowledge that all power and authority come from You, and we are grateful for the privilege to walk in that authority through Christ. Strengthen our faith, Lord, so that it becomes a catalyst for transformation, both in our lives and in the lives of those around us.

Help us to align our hearts with Your will and boldly declare Your promises over our families, workplaces, and ministries. When we face challenges, remind us that You are with us and that no weapon formed against us will prosper.

Lord, teach us to speak life into every situation, to trust in Your Word, and to walk confidently as ambassadors of Your Kingdom. May our faith unlock the full measure of Your power, bringing heaven's solutions to earthly problems.

Use us for Your glory, Father, and let our lives reflect Your love and truth to a world in desperate need of hope.

In Jesus' name, we pray. Amen.

~❖~

Choosing the Voice of Faith

Every day, we face a battle no one else can see. A battle between two voices... One voice feeds fear, doubt, and despair. The other speaks life, truth, and power. Which will you choose?

Discover how the voice of faith changes everything. How one whisper from the Holy Spirit can silence fear, redirect your future, and unlock the power of God in your life. Each day, we are faced with competing voices, fear, doubt, distractions, and the still, unwavering voice of God. Which voice will define your life? For believers, this is not merely a psychological battle; it is spiritual warfare. The voice of

faith, empowered by the Holy Spirit, is God's constant invitation to trust Him fully, even when the path ahead seems unclear.

As Paul described in Romans 7:15, "I do not understand what I do. For what I want to do, I do not do, but what I hate, I do." This tension reveals the daily struggle between our flesh and the Spirit. However, Jesus has given us a Helper in this struggle. He promised in John 14:26, "But the Helper, the Holy Spirit, whom the Father will send in My name, will teach you all things and remind you of everything I have said to you." The Holy Spirit empowers us to hear God's voice, follow His guidance, and walk in faith.

The Voice of Faith: What It Sounds Like

Faith has a distinct sound. It doesn't echo fear, doubt, or confusion; instead, it resonates with God's truth, love, and hope. Here's how it manifests:

1. Faith Sounds Like Truth

➢ When fear says, "You're not enough," faith declares, "I am fearfully and wonderfully made" (Psalm 139:14).

➢ When doubt whispers, "You're alone," faith affirms, "I will never leave you nor forsake you" (Hebrews 13:5).

2. Faith Sounds Like Authority

➢ The voice of faith speaks with heaven's authority. In Mark 4:39, Jesus calmed the storm, saying, "Peace, be still." This same authority is ours when we stand on God's Word.

3. Faith Sounds Like Confidence

➢ When life overwhelms, faith boldly proclaims, "I can do all things through Christ who strengthens me" (Philippians 4:13). Faith shifts our focus from our limitations to God's limitless power.

How to Recognize God's Voice

Just as every dog or cat recognizes the voice of its master, and just as a child can pick out their parent's voice in a crowded room, so should every born-again believer learn to recognize the voice of their Creator, God. His voice is distinct, personal, and unmistakable to those who know Him. Have you noticed? The more quality time you spend with God, in prayer, in His Word, in stillness, the clearer His voice becomes. Like a familiar melody, His guidance becomes easier to hear and harder to ignore. Hearing God's voice requires discernment and practice. Here are biblical principles to guide you:

1. God's Voice Aligns with Scripture

God will never contradict His Word. As Isaiah 40:8 reminds us, "The grass withers and the flowers fall, but the word of our God endures forever."

2. God's Voice Brings Peace

The Holy Spirit's guidance often brings a deep, unshakable peace. Colossians 3:15 says, "Let the peace of Christ rule in your hearts."

3. God's Voice Produces Spiritual Fruit

His words lead to love, joy, peace, patience, kindness, and more (Galatians 5:22-23).

4. God's Voice Draws You Closer to Him

His voice invites intimacy, much like a loving Father calling His child closer.

5. God's Voice is Heard in Stillness

In 1 Kings 19:12, Elijah didn't hear God in the wind, earthquake, or fire, but in a "gentle whisper."

Steps to Hear the Voice of Faith

Tuning into the voice of faith requires intentionality. Here's how you can align your heart and mind to hear God's guidance:

1. Quiet the Noise

- Create daily moments of stillness. Turn off distractions and meditate on God's Word.
- Psalm 46:10 encourages us, "Be still, and know that I am God."

2. Immerse Yourself in Scripture

- Faith is built on the foundation of God's Word. Romans 10:17 says, "Faith comes by hearing, and hearing by the Word of God."

3. Pray for Guidance

- Prayer is not a one-sided conversation but a dialogue with God. In Jeremiah 33:3, God invites us, "Call to me and I will answer you and tell you great and unsearchable things you do not know."

4. Test What You Hear

- Does it align with Scripture? Does it glorify God? Does it bring peace? 1 John 4:1 advises, "Test the spirits to see whether they are from God."

5. Surround Yourself with Godly Community

- Fellowship strengthens faith. Hebrews 10:24-25 reminds us to "spur one another on toward love and good deeds, not giving up meeting together."

6. Obey Promptings Without Delay

* Faith requires action. James 2:26 teaches, "Faith without works is dead."

7. Practice Gratitude and Worship

* Gratitude shifts focus from fear to faith. 1 Thessalonians 5:18 says, "Give thanks in all circumstances; for this is God's will for you."

The Voice of Faith vs. The Voice of Darkness

One of the greatest battles we face as believers of the Lord Jesus Christ is discerning the voice of faith from the voice of darkness. While the Holy Spirit calls us to truth, life, and hope, the enemy seeks to sow confusion, fear, and destruction. Understanding the contrast between these voices equips us to silence the lies of the enemy and walk confidently in God's truth.

What Does the Voice of Darkness Sound Like?

The enemy's voice often mimics our inner doubts and fears, exploiting our insecurities and leading us away from God's promises. Here are some key characteristics:

1. Fear and Doubt

* The enemy's voice thrives on fear, whispering lies that paralyze us and keep us from moving forward.
* For Example: Fear says, "You'll never succeed," while faith proclaims, "I can do all things through Christ who strengthens me" (Philippians 4:13).

2. Condemnation and Shame

* The voice of darkness drags us into guilt and shame over past sins, making us feel unworthy of God's grace.

- Truth: Romans 8:1 reminds us, "There is now no condemnation for those who are in Christ Jesus."

3. Confusion and Chaos

- The enemy's voice creates confusion and disorder, leading us away from clarity and peace.
- Contrast: 1 Corinthians 14:33 says, "For God is not a God of confusion but of peace."

4. Deception and False Promises

- Satan often disguises his lies as half-truths, tempting us with worldly desires and instant gratification.
- Truth: John 8:44 reveals, "When [Satan] lies, he speaks his native language, for he is a liar and the father of lies."

5. Discouragement and Hopelessness

- The enemy seeks to make us feel defeated and powerless, robbing us of the hope we have in Christ.
- Counter: Jeremiah 29:11 declares, "For I know the plans I have for you, declares the Lord, plans for welfare and not for evil, to give you a future and a hope."

The Voice of Faith vs. The Voice of Darkness: Key Contrasts

The Voice of Faith	The Voice of Darkness
Speaks **truth** from God's Word	Speaks **lies** and half-truths
Brings **peace** and clarity	Sows **confusion** and chaos
Encourages **hope** and trust	Feeds **fear** and Discouragement
Calls us to **obedience** and trust	Promotes **disobedience** and rebellion
Inspires **confidence** in God's promises	Breed **doubts** and insecurity

Jesus in the Wilderness

In Matthew 4, Satan tempted Jesus, offering Him worldly power and shortcuts to glory. Each time, Jesus responded with the voice of faith by quoting Scripture:

> ➤ Enemy's Voice: "If you are the Son of God, tell these stones to become bread."

> ➤ Voice of Faith: "It is written, 'Man shall not live on bread alone, but on every word that comes from the mouth of God'" (Matthew 4:4).

Recognizing and Overcoming the Enemy's Voice

1. Identify the Source

- Does the voice align with God's Word? If it contradicts Scripture, it's not from God.
- Isaiah 8:20: "To the law and to the testimony! If they do not speak according to this word, they have no light of dawn."

2. Replace Lies with Truth

- Combat the enemy's lies with the promises of God. Speak Scripture aloud to silence his accusations.
- Ephesians 6:17: "Take the helmet of salvation and the sword of the Spirit, which is the word of God."

3. Pray for Discernment

- Ask the Holy Spirit to help you recognize the difference between His voice and the enemy's deception.
- John 16:13: "But when He, the Spirit of truth, comes, He will guide you into all the truth."

4. Stand Firm in Faith

- Resist the enemy by standing on God's promises, knowing that he must flee.

- James 4:7: "Submit yourselves, then, to God. Resist the devil, and he will flee from you."

Faith Thought:

"The voice of darkness shouts lies to keep you in bondage, but the voice of faith declares freedom and victory through Christ."

By understanding these contrasts, we can better tune our hearts to the voice of faith and silence the enemy's lies. As Psalm 46:10 reminds us, "Be still, and know that I am God." Let us rest in that stillness, trusting God's promises over the noise of doubt and fear.

The Role of the Holy Spirit

The Holy Spirit not only helps us hear God's voice but also intercedes for us. Romans 8:26 assures us, "The Spirit helps us in our weakness. We do not know what we ought to pray for, but the Spirit Himself intercedes for us through wordless groans." Even when we feel weak or uncertain, the Spirit speaks truth and life into our situations.

Faith in Action

Faith is not passive; it's an active trust in God. Consider these takeaways:

1. **Faith Transforms:** Listening to the voice of faith aligns our hearts with God's will.

2. **Faith Speaks Truth:** It silences self-doubt and replaces it with God's promises.

3. **Faith Brings Victory:** Through the Holy Spirit, we overcome inner battles and experience God's power.

4. **Faith Requires Surrender**: Trusting God often means letting go of our plans.

Final Thoughts: A Choice to Make

The battle within is real, but we are not alone. By choosing to listen to the voice of faith, the voice of the Holy Spirit, we unlock God's power and authority in our lives. Let us silence the voices of fear and doubt, replacing them with God's truth.

Psalm 29:4 reminds us, "The voice of the Lord is powerful; the voice of the Lord is majestic." May this voice define your life, guide your decisions, and shape your destiny.

Prayer:

Heavenly Father, thank You for speaking to us through Your Word and Spirit. Help us to silence every voice of doubt and fear and tune into the voice of faith. Empower us to trust You with every detail of our lives. Guide us, Lord, and help us to obey Your promptings with courage and joy. In Jesus' name, Amen.

Faith Declaration:

"The voice of faith is not just a whisper of hope; it carries the authority of heaven. Trust it, obey it, and watch it transform your life."

Heaven in You: The Faith That Defeats Darkness

Never underestimate the power of the measure of faith within you. It is not common, weak, or fragile, it is a divine gift. This faith didn't originate from human strength or a calculated effort on your part. It was born in the very throne room of heaven, breathed into you by the Spirit of God Himself. It's a holy fire that consumes doubt and burns brighter than any darkness you will ever face. It carries the

full weight of God's power, presence, and authority, and that changes everything.

My beloved, you are not walking through life's trials and tribulations alone. Do you not know? The Spirit of the Living God dwells within you. Not only does He reside in you, but He also fills every part of you. His voice speaks, His hand strengthens, His peace calms, and His power flows through you. Faith is much more than belief, it's the living, operative presence of God inside you, unlocking the authority of heaven on earth so that you can do brilliant and wonderful things.

As 1 John 4:4 boldly declares:

"Greater is He that is in you, than he that is in the world."

This promise isn't just a comfort; it's a declaration of victory. It reminds us that the Spirit of God, alive and active in every believer, is infinitely greater than every force of fear, confusion, temptation, envy, or opposition in the world.

Let this truth sink deep:

➢ "Greater is He that is in you." This is the indwelling of the Holy Spirit. By faith, God Himself makes your heart His home. He empowers you, leads you, transforms you, and aligns your life with His will to reveal His glory. Faith opens the door, God walks in, sets up camp, and changes everything from the inside out.

➢ "Than he that is in the world." This refers to the enemy of your soul, Satan, who works through lies, deception, discouragement, and distraction. As my friend, and spiritual giant, the late Dr. Charles Edward Booth once said, "The devil is the author of confusion, but never is he confused." But know this: he is not greater than El Shaddai, the All-Sufficient One.

➢ His power is limited, his influence temporary, and his defeat already sealed. He cannot overcome the authority of the God who lives in you. He has been bankrupt since the beginning of time.

➢ "You are of God" — This is your identity. No one can take that from you. You belong to Him. You are not a product of your past,

your pain, or the boxes others try to place you in. You are God's child, called, chosen, marked by His Spirit, and redeemed by His blood. Your purpose is anchored in His eternal plan.

➤ "And have overcome them." This is your position. You are not waiting for victory; you are living from it. Faith doesn't just help you survive; it positions you to conquer every demonic force that comes against the will of God for your life. You overcome not because of who you are, but because of who is in you, and He never fails.

This kind of supernatural faith is not passive or powerless. It is transformative. It unlocks the power, authority, wisdom, and grace of God in your life to fulfill your calling, defeat every lie, and walk in divine victory. It enables you to rise above fear, defeat, and distraction. It doesn't just hold on; it elevates you and moves mountains. It doesn't just hope, it activates heaven.

Prayer

Lord,

Thank You for the gift of faith, which connects us to Your power and promises. Help us to trust in Your authority and speak Your word over our lives. Like the centurion, teach us to have bold, humble faith that moves mountains. Strengthen our trust in You and help us to see Your hand in every situation. May our faith be a light to others and a testimony of Your goodness. In Jesus' name, Amen.

"Faith untested is faith unproven, but every trial reveals the power of the God who walks through fire with you."

"The testing of your faith produces perseverance."
— James 1:3 (NIV)

Chapter 12
THE TRIALS OF FAITH

Transformative faith is often forged in the fire of significant challenges. Though trials can feel overwhelming, they are divine opportunities to encounter God more intimately.

Challenges, though difficult, are not meant to break us but to build us. They serve as sacred instruments for spiritual growth, purification, and deeper dependence on God. Rather than being obstacles that distance us from Him, trials can become bridges that lead us into His transformative presence.

God doesn't use hardships to harm us, but to shape us. Trials refine our character, deepen our faith, and draw us into closer fellowship with Him.

> *"Consider it pure joy, my brothers and sisters, whenever you face trials of many kinds, because you know that the testing of your faith produces perseverance." (James 1:2–3)*

> *"And we know that in all things God works for the good of those who love him, who have been called according to his purpose."* *(Romans 8:28)*

Through trials, God shapes us to become more like Christ. Just as gold is purified by fire, our faith is refined through adversity.

> *"He will sit as a refiner and purifier of silver; he will purify the Levites and refine them like gold and silver." (Malachi 3:3)*

Instead of seeing trials as walls that separate us from God, we should view them as sacred invitations into His presence. These moments of difficulty remind us of our dependency on Him and draw us nearer to His heart.

> *"The Lord is near to the brokenhearted and saves the crushed in spirit." (Psalm 34:18)*

> *"Cast all your anxiety on him because he cares for you."* (1 Peter 5:7)

Every trial invites us to seek God for wisdom, strength, and comfort—opening the door to a deeper relationship with Him. "Call to me and I will answer you and tell you great and unsearchable things you do not know." (Jeremiah 33:3)

Challenges as Opportunities for Transformation

Trials are not merely hurdles to overcome—they are divine opportunities for God to transform us. When we trust Him through adversity, His power operates in and through our lives.

> *"But he said to me, 'My grace is sufficient for you, for my power is made perfect in weakness.' Therefore, I will boast all the more gladly about my weaknesses, so that Christ's power may rest on me." (2 Corinthians 12:9)*

> *"And the God of all grace... after you have suffered a little while, will himself restore you and make you strong, firm and steadfast." (1 Peter 5:10)*

God never wastes our pain. Every hardship is a vessel through which He matures our faith, glorifies Himself, and fulfills His divine purposes.

How Trials Purify and Mature Faith

The Apostle Peter reminds us:

> *"These trials will show that your faith is genuine. It is being tested as fire tests and purifies gold—though your faith is far more precious than mere gold." (1 Peter 1:7, NLT)*

Like a goldsmith uses fire to remove impurities, God uses trials to refine our faith. Adversity exposes our fears, doubts, and misplaced trust, yet, as we endure, these are stripped away, leaving a stronger and more steadfast belief.

Rather than viewing trials as punishments, we can see them as divine refining processes, opportunities for God to deepen our trust and prepare us for His greater purposes.

Biblical Examples of Faith Through Trials

The Bible gives powerful testimonies of those whose faith was refined through hardship:

➤ Job:
After losing everything, Job declared,
"Though he slay me, yet will I hope in him." (Job 13:15)
His faith endured, and God restored him, blessing him even more than before.

➤ Joseph:
Betrayed, enslaved, and imprisoned unjustly, Joseph still trusted God.
"You intended to harm me, but God intended it for good..." (Genesis 50:20)
His suffering led to the salvation of nations.

➤ Paul:
Beaten, imprisoned, shipwrecked, Paul's life was marked by suffering.
"We also glory in our sufferings, because we know that suf-

fering produces perseverance; perseverance, character; and character, hope." (Romans 5:3-4)

His trials only intensified his mission and faith.

These examples remind us: Trials are not the end; they are the process through which God prepares us for more.

Trusting God Through Hardship

Enduring trials with faith transforms us. When difficulty arises, it challenges us to trust in God's character, purpose, and promises.

1. Focus on God's Character:

Know who God is, faithful, loving, and sovereign. Meditate on passages like Psalm 23 and Romans 8:28 to anchor your soul in truth.

2. Embrace God's Purpose in Trials:

Hardships are not random.

> *"Consider it pure joy... because you know that the testing of your faith produces perseverance." (James 1:2-4)*

3. Hold On to God's Promises:

Cling to His Word.

> *"Do not fear, for I am with you... I will strengthen you and help you." (Isaiah 41:10)*

Refined by Fire, Strengthened by Faith

Faith that transforms is not born in ease, it is forged in trials, matured through perseverance, and empowered by trust in God's promises.

As with Job, Joseph, and Paul, our trials are not meant to destroy us but to refine us, unlocking God's power in new and profound ways.

When you face trials, remember they are part of God's refining process. These are sacred moments where you can witness another dimension of God's power, presence, and promises.

God is not limited by space or time. He works across dimensions beyond our understanding. When you go through trials with a faithful heart, you gain a deeper revelation of who He is.

If you ever meet someone deeply committed to Christ, look closely at the trials they've endured, their faith was likely forged in fire.

Final Encouragement

Trials are not the end of your story; they are the very means through which God transforms your faith. By trusting His purposes, persevering through hardship, and embracing His promises, you will emerge stronger, wiser, and more prepared for His calling.

Your challenges are not barriers to God. They are invitations to encounter Him in ways you never imagined.

Let every trial lead you deeper into His love and further into your destiny.

> *"Faith that transforms doesn't just survive hardship, it thrives in it, revealing God's power and preparing us for His eternal purposes."*

Permission Granted

"As our challenges and chaos increase, so too must our faith grow."

To understand this statement, it refers to the notion that faith is not merely about peace in difficult times but a strength that grows precisely through difficulty and uncertainty. What grows out of faith?

When life is calm and everything is manageable, we often don't feel the same need to depend on faith. As challenges mount and circumstances become overwhelming, we are pushed beyond our own abil-

ities and control. It is when faith becomes essential. In times of chaos, when outcomes are uncertain, and our resources are stretched, faith offers both an anchor and a compass. It anchors us with the reassurance that there is a purpose beyond the present difficulties and serves as a compass, pointing us toward resilience and trust.

The statement, "He may not come when you want Him, but He is always right on time," speaks to the profound trust that faith calls us to have in God's timing, even when it feels different from our own. This classic saying in the Baptist tradition reminds us that, while we may have our own hopes, deadlines, and expectations, God operates on a divine timetable that sees beyond our immediate circumstances. He knows exactly when and how to step in for the greatest impact and purpose.

When we declare, "I will wait on God, for my victory is within reach," we are making a powerful statement of faith. It's an acknowledgment that while our desires may feel urgent, they may not always align with God's perfect timing, and that's okay. Trusting in His timing is not a passive resignation; it's an active confidence that He is sovereign, wise, and good.

Waiting on God doesn't mean we sit idly or abandon hope. It means we remain steadfast in prayer, faithful in action, and confident in His promises, even when the path ahead is unclear. It means believing that God is working behind the scenes, orchestrating events, opening and closing doors, and shaping us in the process. He is strengthening our character, refining our purpose, and aligning the pieces in ways we may not fully understand right now.

That is the beauty of divine timing. It reassures us that we are not forgotten or overlooked. Rather, we are being prepared for something greater than we could achieve on our own. Our waiting becomes a testimony of trust.

This is good news: God is not distant. He is intimately aware of our needs, deeply invested in our journey, and actively working within and around us. His supernatural power is constantly at work, not

only for His glory but also for the fulfillment of His divine purpose in and through us.

This kind of faith asks us to release the pressure of the "when" and "how" to God, knowing that delays don't mean denial. In fact, God's timing often brings blessings and growth we couldn't have achieved otherwise. So even in moments of waiting or uncertainty, faith reminds us to hold on, to be patient, and to trust that our victory is indeed within reach. Because while God may seem to come at the final hour, His arrival is never late, it's right on time, bringing the victory, strength, and fulfillment we need.

Imagine someone telling you that you could walk on water, not just metaphorically, but truly defy the laws of nature and step boldly into the impossible. Not just the waters of the Chesapeake Bay, but challenges and dreams that lie far beyond the scope of your current thinking. What would your response be? Would you scoff in disbelief? Or would you have the faith to believe that, with God, all things are possible?

The story of Peter walking on water with Jesus is, in many ways, our story too. It is an invitation for every believer in Jesus Christ to step beyond the confines of comfort, beyond our limited and often rigid views of God's power and authority. It calls us to open our eyes to the limitless possibilities available through faith, a power not restricted by human logic or fear.

Faith is the bridge between what we know and what we cannot yet see, between earthly limits and divine potential. But what gives a believer the boldness to step into the miraculous, to imagine a future shaped by God's promises rather than present circumstances? It is God's grace that gives us permission, His divine favor that empowers us to dream, to act, and to walk where reason says we cannot.

INSIGHTS:

1. Walking on Water: What Does It Mean?

When Jesus walked on water in Matthew 14:22-33, it was a powerful demonstration of His divine authority over nature. But when Peter saw Jesus doing this, he asked for permission to join Him on the waves. Peter knew that to walk on water, he needed Jesus' authority, he couldn't step out of the boat without it. This story symbolizes the faith required to venture into areas where human strength alone is insufficient, where one must rely fully on God. What gives us the authority to act with faith in our situation?

> ➤ **Scripture:** "Then Peter got down out of the boat, walked on the water, and came toward Jesus." — Matthew 14:29

> ➤ **Insight:** Stepping into the unknown, Peter wasn't relying on his ability but on the authority, Jesus granted him. This teaches us that faith isn't about ignoring reality; it's about trusting God's reality over our own.

2. What Does the Water Represent?

Water represents everything that is beyond our control—our doubts, fears, challenges, and the unknown. By stepping onto the water, Peter trusted Jesus' invitation over his natural instincts and fears. When we trust in God's authority, we, too, can "walk on water", overcoming obstacles and doing the things that would be impossible in our own strength.

> ➤ **Scripture:** "I can do all things through Christ who strengthens me." — Philippians 4:13

> ➤ **Insight:** Like Peter, we're called to trust God's strength rather than our limitations. Walking on water isn't just about the miraculous; it's about letting God's authority guide us through every challenge.

3. Faith in God's Authority

Faith in God allows us to step beyond our human understanding and limitations. Jesus said in John 14:12, "Very truly I tell you, whoever believes in me will do the works I have been doing, and they will do even greater things than these, because I am going to the Father." Jesus is explaining that those who believe in Him can, by His authority, carry out His works, even greater things, through the power of His name. He granted believers the permission to be agents of His authority on earth.

> **Scripture**: "Now faith is confidence in what we hope for and assurance about what we do not see." — Hebrews 11:1

> **Insight:** Faith moves us from just believing in the possible to trusting in the unimaginable, with God's authority empowering each step.

4. What Does Faith in God's Authority Allow Us to Do?

Faith gives believers the permission to do the impossible, but this isn't about personal glory. It's about acting in alignment with God's purposes and reflecting His glory. When we operate under God's authority, He uses us to bring healing, restoration, hope, and love to a broken world.

Examples:

> **Healing the Sick:** By praying in faith and in Jesus' name, we can intercede for the sick and see healing, as Jesus instructed (James 5:15).

> **Loving the Unlovable:** Faith in God's love allows us to love others radically, even when it's difficult (John 13:34-35).

> **Living Courageously:** Faith allows us to step out and serve boldly, facing fears and challenges, trusting God's guidance (2 Timothy 1:7).

5. The Source of Our Authority: The Name of Jesus

Yes, it is in the name of Jesus that believers have permission to do the impossible. The name of Jesus is powerful because it represents His authority, character, and the divine connection to God the Father. When we act in His name, we are standing not in our strength but in His sovereign authority.

> ➢ **Scripture:** "And I will do whatever you ask in my name, so that the Father may be glorified in the Son." — John 14:13

> ➢ **Insight:** By invoking Jesus' name, we're not demanding our desires; we're aligning with His will and allowing His power to work through us.

"Faith allows for possibilities"

"Faith teaches us that sometimes, when we reach the very end of what we can handle, when we're holding on by the thinnest thread, our instinct is to grip tighter, to tie a knot in that rope and cling for dear life. But true faith asks something unexpected: it asks us to *let go*. Why? Because faith is about trust. Faith says, "Even if I can't see what's below, even if it feels like I'm in freefall, I believe that God will catch me.""

This is not the surrender of defeat, but a powerful act of trust. When we let go, we're acknowledging that our strength alone isn't enough, but God's is. It's an invitation for God to step in, to lift us, to carry us through what we cannot carry on our own. Faith isn't about having all the answers or holding it together. It's the willingness to say, "God, I trust You to take it from here." Have you ever experienced trusting someone so completely that you just let go of everything? Allow God to be that someone.

Letting go becomes an act of courage and surrender, a choice to believe that God's hands are right there, stronger and more secure than anything we could hold onto ourselves. When we let go in faith, we open ourselves to experience His power, His grace, and His guidance in ways we could never see when we're holding on too tightly.

What It Takes to Walk on Water (Spiritually):

1. Faith in God's Authority: Trust that He can do the impossible through you.

2. Courage to Step Out: Take action even when it feels risky.

3. Focus on Jesus: Keep your eyes on Him to stay steady amid challenges.

4. Act in His Name: Align with God's purpose and trust in the power of Jesus' name.

In conclusion, just as Jesus granted Peter permission to walk on water, He also grants us permission to step into His power and authority. But stepping out in faith requires trust, humility, and surrender. We cannot accomplish these things by our own strength, but only by embracing the authority that Jesus freely offers. When we say, **"Permission Granted,"** we're accepting God's invitation to live beyond limitations and to walk into the fullness of what He has planned. As Jesus said, "Whoever believes in me will do the works I have been doing, and they will do even greater things than these." The question is: are you ready to step out of the boat?

When life collapses like a bridge, faith becomes the structure that carries us to safety. Trust in God, step out in faith, and watch as He transforms your life.

When Hope Calls, Faith Answers

Faith is the bridge between our present struggles and God's miraculous power. It's not merely a belief, it's a trust so deep it compels action, even when logic tells us otherwise. Hebrews 11:1 reminds us, *"Faith is the substance of things hoped for, the evidence of things not seen."* Faith opens the door to divine authority and allows God to work through our lives for lasting change.

Today, we'll journey into the story of a Roman centurion, a man of surprising faith who trusted in Jesus' authority and witnessed a

miracle that transformed lives. His story teaches us that faith is not bound by position, nationality, or circumstance.

In Luke 7:1–10, we meet a Roman centurion, a man of status and influence. He was a military officer, overseeing a hundred soldiers. He wasn't a Jew and lived outside the covenant community of Israel. Yet, his story reveals a faith so profound that Jesus marveled at it.

The centurion had a servant whom he deeply cared for, a rarity in his time. This servant was gravely ill and near death. The centurion had likely exhausted every resource, but nothing could save the man he valued so much. Yet, this Roman soldier had heard of Jesus, of His healing power, authority, and compassion. Though a Gentile, the centurion believed that Jesus had the power to heal, even from a distance.

Instead of demanding Jesus' attention, the centurion sent Jewish elders to plead on his behalf, saying, *"Lord, do not trouble Yourself, for I do not deserve to have You come under my roof. That is why I did not even consider myself worthy to come to You. But say the word, and my servant will be healed"* (Luke 7:6-7).

The centurion recognized something extraordinary: Jesus' authority was absolute. As a man who commanded soldiers, he understood the power of orders and submission. He believed that if Jesus spoke healing into existence, it would happen, regardless of proximity.

When Jesus heard this, He marveled, turning to the crowd and saying, *"I tell you, I have not found such great faith even in Israel"* (Luke 7:9). At that moment, the servant was healed.

The centurion's story reveals a faith grounded in humility and recognition of Jesus' divine authority. His trust in Christ's word demonstrates that faith operates in a separate realm, one governed entirely by God. The centurion didn't need to see signs or evidence; he believed in the power of God's spoken word.

Faith, like the centurion's, moves mountains because it aligns with God's will and authority. As Jesus said in Matthew 8:13, *"Go! Let it*

be done just as you believed it would." Faith doesn't demand proof; it simply believes and trusts in God's power.

Faith as a Bridge to God's Power

Much like the Francis Scott Key Bridge in Baltimore, Maryland, faith serves as a connection between two places: the impossible and the miraculous. The centurion was on one side, facing hopelessness, helplessness, and human limitations. But faith became the bridge that carried him to healing and transformation.

What made this faith remarkable? It wasn't rooted in physical proximity to Jesus or years of religious study. It was grounded in an understanding that Jesus' authority transcended physical space and human limits. The centurion's faith reminds us that God's power isn't constrained by our circumstances or boundaries.

The story of Julio Cervantes Suarez, the lone survivor of the Francis Scott Key Bridge collapse, reflects the same faith under extraordinary pressure. Trapped in the icy waters of the Patapsco River, surrounded by death and destruction, Julio called on God with a heart full of faith.

Faith is like a bridge; it connects you to the promises of God. The Francis Scott Key Bridge once served as a vital link, carrying thousands of vehicles each day. It stood as a symbol of connection and purpose until the unthinkable happened. On March 26, 2024, a cargo ship lost power and struck one of its main supports. In an instant, the bridge collapsed, taking lives, disrupting livelihoods, and shattering stability.

Amidst the turmoil, Julio Cervantes Suarez, one of the workers on the bridge, found himself immersed in the frigid waters of the Patapsco River. His truck had plunged into the waters below, and death seemed imminent. Yet, even in the darkness, he found himself clinging to a debris-filled lifeline. Faith became his bridge to survival, carrying him from despair to deliverance.

Julio later recounted how he cried out to God in that moment: *"I asked Him to take care of my wife and kids. And I asked for forgiveness for everything I've done."* Faith became his anchor when the odds were against him. Though he didn't know how to swim, he held on until rescuers arrived. His survival defied logic, and his testimony became a beacon of hope.

Like the centurion, Julio couldn't rely on his own strength to save him. He prayed, asking God to forgive him and take care of his family. Holding onto debris, with no ability to swim, Julio's faith became his lifeline. Against all odds, he was rescued.

Both the centurion and Julio faced situations beyond human control. Their faith bridged the gap to God's power, transforming despair into hope.

What the Centurion Teaches Us About Faith

1. **Faith Is Humble**. The centurion, despite his high status, approached Jesus with humility. He acknowledged his unworthiness and trusted in Christ's authority.

   ▪ *"God opposes the proud but shows favor to the humble" (James 4:6).*

2. **Faith Trusts in God's Word.** The centurion didn't need Jesus to come physically to his home. He trusted that a single word from Jesus would bring healing.

   ▪ *"So then faith comes by hearing, and hearing by the word of God" (Romans 10:17).*

3. **Faith Is Rooted in God's Authority.** The centurion's military background helped him understand Jesus' divine authority. He believed that God's commands could transcend time, space, and circumstance.

   ▪ *"For the word of God is alive and active. Sharper than any double-edged sword" (Hebrews 4:12).*

4. **Faith Moves God to Act**. Jesus marveled at the centurion's faith, and his servant was healed. Faith isn't about the size of our efforts but the depth of our trust in God.

   ※ *"If you have faith as small as a mustard seed, you can say to this mountain, 'Move from here to there,' and it will move" (Matthew 17:20).*

Faith That Transforms Lives

Faith, like the centurion's, transforms lives. It gives us access to God's authority and power, enabling us to experience miracles and breakthroughs. When we trust in Him fully, we step into His divine purpose and see the impossible become possible.

The centurion's story reminds us that faith is not about our qualifications or circumstances. It's about recognizing who God is and believing that He can do all things.

In conclusion, when hope calls, let your faith answer. Like the centurion, trust in the authority of Jesus. Like Julio, hold onto faith even when it feels like there's nothing else to cling to. Faith isn't about understanding every detail, it's about trusting the One who does.

Faith transforms. It bridges the gap between your current reality and God's promises. It moves mountains, restores lives, and unlocks the power of God's word.

As Jesus said in John 14:13-14, *"And I will do whatever you ask in My name, so that the Father may be glorified in the Son. You may ask me for anything in my name, and I will do it."*

*"Faith is not just believing for what you want—
it's surrendering to what God has planned and
trusting it is better."*

"Not my will, but Yours, be done."
— Luke 22:42 (NKJV)

Chapter 13
THE ROLE OF OBEDIENCE

Obedience is the bridge that connects our faith to God's purpose, aligning our will with His perfect plan. It is through obedience that we demonstrate our love and trust in God, creating the pathway for His blessings, guidance, and transformative power to flow into our lives. As Jesus said, "If you love me, you will keep my commandments" (John 14:15).

Obedience to God is not a passive action; it is the active practice of living out His commands and walking by faith. It involves:

➢ **Engaging with Scripture:** Regularly reading and understanding the Bible (Psalm 119:105).

➢ **Following Jesus' Teachings:** Applying His words in every area of life (Matthew 7:24-25).

➢ **Serving Others:** Demonstrating Christ's love through acts of kindness and service (Galatians 5:13).

➢ **Living with Grace:** Treating others with respect and humility (Colossians 4:6).

➢ **Worship and Gratitude:** Thanking God in prayer and song for His goodness (Psalm 100:4).

➢ **Fellowship:** Participating in church to grow in community and faith (Hebrews 10:24-25).

When we walk in obedience, we experience profound spiritual growth and transformation. Obedience:

➢ Teaches us to discern right from wrong (Hebrews 5:14).

➢ Strengthens us to resist temptations (James 4:7).

➢ Builds deeper relationships with God and others (John 15:10-11).

➢ Fosters confidence and security in His promises (Proverbs 3:5-6).

➢ Unlocks God's creative purpose for our lives (Ephesians 2:10).

➢ Leads us into His promises, such as His protection and peace (Psalm 121:7-8).

As the Apostle John writes, "This is how we know that we love the children of God: by loving God and carrying out His commands. In fact, this is love for God: to keep His commands. And His commands are not burdensome, for everyone born of God overcomes the world" (1 John 5:2-4).

Through obedience, we deepen our faith, grow in love, and live in alignment with God's perfect will, fulfilling the calling He has placed on our lives.

Faith that transforms is not passive, it requires action. True faith compels us to align our will with God's and take tangible steps of obedience. It is through obedience that we unlock the power and authority of God for lasting change, both in our own lives and in the world around us.

Faith without works is dead. Faith is the foundation of our walk with God, but without action, it remains incomplete. James 2:17 declares, *"Faith by itself, if it is not accompanied by action, is dead."* Faith without obedience is like a car without fuel—it cannot move forward or fulfill its purpose.

Abraham's story exemplifies this truth. When God called him to sacrifice Isaac, Abraham's obedience demonstrated his unwavering trust. James writes, *"You see that his faith and his actions were working together, and his faith was made complete by what he did"* (James 2:22).

Abraham's obedience unlocked God's power, and his faith transformed him into the father of many nations.

Faith that transforms is a living, active faith that responds to God's Word. It is not enough to say we trust God; our actions must reflect that trust, even when obedience feels challenging or requires great sacrifice.

How does submission unlocks God's promises? Obedience is not about earning God's favor but stepping into the blessings He has already prepared for us. Submission to His will positions us to receive His promises and experience His power in our lives.

1. **Provision:** God equips those who obey Him. When the Israelites obeyed God's instructions to gather manna in the wilderness, He faithfully provided for them each day (Exodus 16:4).

2. **Protection:** Obedience keeps us in the center of God's will, safeguarding us from the consequences of disobedience. Proverbs 3:5-6 assures us that as we trust and submit to God, He directs our paths.

3. **Purpose:** Obedience allows us to fulfill God's unique purpose for our lives. Jeremiah 29:11 reminds us that His plans are for our good, to prosper us and give us hope.

The greatest blessing of obedience, however, is intimacy with God. Jesus said, *"If you love me, keep my commands"* (John 14:15). Obedience strengthens our relationship with Him, allowing us to experience His presence and guidance more fully.

Let's examine a few biblical examples with Noah and Jonah's lessons in obedience.

➤ **Noah:**

Noah's obedience in building the ark, despite the ridicule and uncertainty, demonstrates the power of unwavering faith. By following God's specific instructions, Noah became a vessel for salvation, preserving his family and the creatures of the earth. His story reminds

us that obedience often requires perseverance and trust in what we cannot yet see.

> **Jonah:**

In contrast, Jonah's disobedience led to turmoil—not just for himself but for those around him. However, God's mercy gave him a second chance. When Jonah finally obeyed and delivered God's message to Nineveh, an entire city repented and was saved. Jonah's story shows that while disobedience delays God's plan, it cannot thwart it.

Both Noah and Jonah illustrate that obedience is not always easy, but it is always necessary. Whether through steadfast compliance or lessons learned from resistance, God uses our choices to fulfill His purposes.

Obedience starts with discerning God's will and taking deliberate steps to follow it. Here's how to align your actions with His plan:

1. Seek God in Prayer and Scripture:

The Bible is God's divine roadmap for our lives. Regularly reading and meditating on His Word helps us understand His commands and recognize His voice.

2. Be Attentive to the Holy Spirit:

The Holy Spirit often speaks through inner convictions, godly counsel, or circumstances. Cultivate a listening heart and be open to His leading, even when it challenges your comfort zone.

3. Act Immediately:

Delayed obedience is disobedience. When God prompts you to act—whether it's forgiving someone, stepping into a new role, or making a change—respond with urgency and faith.

4. Stay Accountable:

Share your journey with trusted believers who can encourage and challenge you to remain faithful to God's instructions.

5. Reflect and Adjust:

Journaling can help you process your obedience journey and recognize areas where you need to grow. Reflect on how God's faithfulness has met your steps of obedience in the past.

Faith that transforms through obedience is faith that obeys. It is faith in action, surrendering our will to God and trusting Him to lead. Obedience not only strengthens our faith but also unlocks God's power and authority in our lives, bringing lasting change.

Like Noah, we are called to obey even when the task seems overwhelming, or the outcome unclear. Like Jonah, we may struggle with resistance, but God's grace invites us to realign with His plan.

By aligning our will with God's, we step into the fullness of His promises, experience His blessings, and become vessels of His transformative power. Faith without works is dead, but faith expressed through obedience brings life, purpose, and the authority to impact the world for His glory.

Obedience is the bridge between faith and transformation. By aligning your actions with God's will, you not only demonstrate trust in Him but also unlock His blessings and power. Faith that obeys is faith that thrives, bringing lasting change to your life and the world around you.

~❖~

Faith: The Master Key to the Supernatural

There are certain things in life, deep, spiritual realities, that those who do not know Jesus Christ as Lord and Savior will never truly grasp. That's because spiritual truth isn't processed through the nat-

ural mind; it must be revealed by the Spirit of God. Paul explains this clearly:

> *"But the natural man receiveth not the things of the Spirit of God: for they are foolishness unto him: neither can he know them, because they are spiritually discerned." (1 Corinthians 2:14, KJV)*

Let me give you a real-life example. I've had conversations with people who still believe God is just "the man upstairs", distant, disconnected, and impersonal. I know you've met people like that too. In my mind, I picture them thinking the world is still flat, not in the geographical sense, but in the rigidity of their thinking about Christ. It reflects either ignorance or a lack of opportunity to experience a personal relationship with the Creator of heaven and earth. Spiritually speaking, they're locked into a limited framework. The enemy of darkness has blinded their eyes, preventing them from truly seeing their need for God. They see the surface but miss the substance. It's like trying to fix a spiritual issue with a toolbox full of natural tools, if all you have is a hammer, everything looks like a nail. But the supernatural realm requires more than human reasoning. It requires revelation, discernment, and above all, faith.

Faith is not a blind leap into the unknown; it is a bold step into the marvelous light. It's the ability God gives every believer to see beyond what is visible, to understand what defies logic, and to access what is humanly impossible.

> Faith is heaven's lens, adjusting our earthly perspective.

Through it, we believe that God spoke the cosmos into existence, that from nothing came everything (Genesis 1). To those without faith, that sounds like fantasy. But to those who walk with God, it's the most powerful truth imaginable.

Doubt, on the other hand, isn't just hesitation, it's a spiritual blockade. Doubt causes chaos and confusion, hindering the divine influence of God in our lives. Where faith opens the gate, doubt locks it every time. You could say that faith is the divine hinge on the door to

the supernatural. When it swings open, heaven invades earth. Faith gives us access, not because we're worthy, but because we believe in the One who is.

This kind of faith isn't passive. It's active, it's alive, and it's transformative. It doesn't just shift our thinking; it reorders our living. It moves us from theory to spiritual authority. Walking by faith allows you to respond with intention rather than reacting impulsively, thereby enabling you to take control of your circumstances.

Look at Abraham. God promised him descendants as numerous as the stars, even though he was nearly 100 and Sarah had been barren her whole life. The facts shouted "impossible," but faith heard something different:

> "Against all hope, Abraham in hope believed... without weakening in his faith." (Romans 4:18–20)

He didn't deny the facts, he defied them by anchoring his trust in God's ability, not his own limitations. Faith redefined his reality according to God's authority.

Faith doesn't submit to time, space, or matter. It operates in a dimension where those rules no longer apply. Why? Because faith comes from God, and God is not subject to the laws He Himself created. Jesus said:

> "If you have faith as small as a mustard seed... nothing will be impossible for you." (Matthew 17:20)

Faith is not bound by the natural; it enforces the laws of the Kingdom.

When you live by faith, you don't just see what is, you begin to see what could be according to God's will. The "impossible" becomes an invitation to watch God move.

Here's a practical example: Imagine receiving a terminal diagnosis. The facts say it's over. But faith hears a different report:

> *"By His stripes you are healed." (Isaiah 53:5)*

Faith doesn't ignore the diagnosis; it overrides it with divine truth. That's not denial. That's supernatural living.

Faith removes limits. It doesn't wait for the future; it lives in the power of God's "now." God can bless you now, heal you now, deliver you now, set you free now. That's the beauty of faith. It reaches into eternity and pulls heaven into your present moment.

In the spiritual realm, faith is the master key that unlocks what others cannot even see:

➢ The Favor of God – Faith positions you for divine preference. Like Joseph, who rose from prison to palace—not because of luck, but because of favor.

Modern example? You apply for a job you're underqualified for, but the employer says, "There's just something about you." That's favor, unearned, undeserved, undeniable (Genesis 39:21). How it's released: Favor is God's sovereign hand in action. His authority opens doors no one can shut. Faith walks into what God has already prepared.

➢ The Peace of God – Faith anchors you in the storm. Picture a single mother, unsure how she'll feed her children, yet worshipping in the kitchen because she knows Jehovah Jireh will provide. Peace isn't from circumstances; it comes from knowing the God who reigns above them (Mark 4:39–40).

How it's released: God speaks peace through His Word. Faith receives that peace and resists every demonic spirit that tries to steal it.

➢ Joy Unspeakable – Faith celebrates before the victory. Paul and Silas sang in prison, not because they were free, but because they were faithful (Acts 16:25).

How it's released: Joy is a fruit of the Spirit, ignited by God's presence. Faith activates joy by looking beyond the trial and rejoicing in the victory God has declared.

➢ Healing and Deliverance – The woman with the issue of blood didn't just touch Jesus—her faith pulled healing from Him. "Daughter, your faith has made you well." (Mark 5:34)

How it's released: Healing is God's authority over sickness in action. Faith connects our need with His power.

➢ Wisdom and Revelation – Faith opens the mind to receive what logic cannot grasp.

Why? Because expectation honors God (James 1:5–6). How it's released: When you ask in faith, the Spirit reveals mysteries that transcend intellect and unveil Kingdom truth.

➢ Destiny and Purpose – Faith says yes when everything else says no. Moses didn't feel qualified, but faith stepped into destiny anyway.

Your calling may not come with clarity, but faith declares, "If God called me, He'll carry me."

As my former pastor, Bishop Walter S. Thomas, Sr., used to say: "If God gives you the vision, He will also provide the provision." How it's released: Faith embraces the call and trusts that God will equip and provide, even when the path is unclear.

➢ The Presence of God – Above all, faith draws us near to Him. It has a magnetic pull.

"Without faith, it is impossible to please God." (Hebrews 11:6) Not because God is harsh, but because faith is the language of relationship. It says, "I trust You even when I can't trace You." As I've prayed, "I trust You, Lord, more than I trust myself." How it's released: God responds to faith with closeness. His Spirit inhabits the space created by trust.

So how is this kind of faith even possible?

Because it doesn't originate from within us, it comes from above. It is not acquired through willpower; it is bestowed by divine grace

(Ephesians 2:8). Faith is the breath of heaven in the lungs of earth. God's life flowing through us to do what we never could on our own.

Faith that transforms and unlocks God's authority is rooted in supernatural belief. It's how we partner with God to move mountains, walk on water, heal the sick, speak life into dead places, and shift atmospheres wherever we go. It's how we live, not by what we see, but by who we know.

Faith That Transforms by Yielding to God's Authority

You cannot talk about faith that transforms without recognizing faith as a shield, and you cannot separate that shield from your willingness to yield to God. Faith that unlocks God's power is directly tied to your surrender. The more you yield, the more power is released. No yielding, no power.

As a believer in Jesus Christ, have you considered that God's limitless power and supreme authority are not distant theological concepts, but living realities waiting to be activated by your faith? Faith isn't passive belief; it is an active surrender that opens the door to divine power. It's the key that engages God's spiritual provision in every part of your life.

With Faith That Transforms, we see that faith isn't just a helpful tool in the Christian life, it is the activating force that unleashes the armor of God, positions you under divine authority, and ushers in supernatural protection, provision, and victory.

Faith That Unlocks the Full Armor of God

In Ephesians 6:10–17, Paul outlines the "whole armor of God", a divine strategy for spiritual warfare. Central to this armor is the shield of faith:

> "In all circumstances take up the shield of faith, with which you can extinguish all the flaming darts of the evil one" (Ephesians 6:16, ESV).

This isn't poetic language, it's theological reality. Faith is how God's power is activated, and His authority becomes real in your life. Without faith, the armor is present, but powerless, divinely designed, but spiritually dormant. But when faith is engaged, the armor becomes alive, dynamic, and unshakable.

When you take up the shield of faith, no matter what life throws at you, the enemy has no chance. Because this shield isn't from you, it's backed by Heaven.

What Is the Shield of Faith?

The shield of faith is not just a defensive object. It is a spiritual force field fueled by your trust in who God is, what He has said, and what He has promised. It is divine confidence. It deflects fiery darts like fear, doubt, temptation, accusation, and deception, not by your might, but by your faith in God's authority and His Word.

It doesn't run on human willpower. It runs on spiritual surrender. The shield of faith works when you yield, when you align your life with God's truth and trust His hand above your understanding.

The Shield of Faith in Action

Faith doesn't only stop what's coming at you, it also stops what's rising up within you. Sometimes, your greatest enemy isn't external, it's your own desires, emotions, or impulses that conflict with God's will.

That's why doors you keep pulling on won't open. They're not locked by accident; they're sealed by divine protection. Faith doesn't just block Satan's attacks; it filters your life decisions, guarding you from self-sabotage.

Isaiah 54:17 says, "No weapon formed against you shall prosper." Faith ensures the weapon doesn't form fully, whether it's forged in hell, hurled by people, or born in your own heart.

To live by faith is to live under God's rule. When you take up the shield of faith, you don't just avoid defeat, you walk in supernatural authority. You don't just survive spiritual battles, you dominate them, clothed in the full power of God.

Faith is not a feeling. It is a force. And that force is activated when you yield.

This is the kind of faith that transforms.

This is how you unlock the power and authority of God in your life.

This is the faith that makes warriors out of worshipers.

A Prayer for Transformative Faith

Heavenly Father, thank You for being the God of the impossible. Help us to place our trust in You, knowing that our limitations are no match for Your limitless power. May our faith bear fruit that reflects Your Spirit within us, and may our lives be a testimony of Your goodness and grace. Use us, Lord, to fulfill Your purposes in ways we cannot yet see. In Jesus' name, Amen.

"The impossible is simply the starting line for a faith that believes nothing is too hard for God."

"With God all things are possible."
— Matthew 19:26 (KJV)

Chapter 14
FAITH FOR THE IMPOSSIBLE

Faith is more than belief; it is the divine key that unlocks the supernatural power and authority of God in our lives. Faith bridges the gap between heaven and earth, enabling the miraculous to invade the natural. It's not rooted in wishful thinking or blind optimism; it is grounded in the unchanging character of God and aligned with His sovereign will.

True faith for the impossible doesn't beg, it believes. It clings to God's Word, draws strength from His presence, and boldly declares:

"My God is able. My God is willing. And even if He chooses not to move how I expect, I will still trust Him like never before."

This kind of faith doesn't deny reality, it defies it. It stares down sickness, storms, lack, fear, and impossibility, and still proclaims God's supreme authority:

> *"With man this is impossible, but with God all things are possible."*
> *(Matthew 19:26)*

When we fully embrace the nature of God and surrender to His authority, our faith rises, and miracles follow. The atmosphere shifts. Heaven's reality invades earth.

Faith Is Built on the Character of God

To walk in faith for the impossible, we must truly know the One we trust. Faith grows not from religious effort, but from divine intimacy.

The more we understand who God is, the more confidence we gain in His ability, and His desire, to move on our behalf.

God's character isn't just the foundation of faith, it's the fuel that sustains it. Knowing who He is empowers us to pray boldly, believe confidently, and stand unwaveringly.

Let's reflect on the God who makes the impossible possible:

God Is Love

His love isn't distant or passive — it is personal, relentless, and sacrificial. His love finds us in darkness and lifts us into radiant hope.

> *"God is love, and whoever abides in love abides in God, and God abides in him." (1 John 4:16)*

God Is Holy

He is set apart — flawless in purity, radiant in righteousness. And yet, He draws us near with mercy.

> *"There is no one holy like the Lord; there is no one besides you; there is no Rock like our God." (1 Samuel 2:2)*

God Is All-Powerful

Nothing is too hard for Him. He speaks, and creation responds. He commands, and even death surrenders.

> *"Ah, Sovereign Lord... Nothing is too hard for you." (Jeremiah 32:17)*

God Is Always Present

In your valley, in your hospital room, in your silent tears , He is near.

> *"Where can I go from your Spirit? Where can I flee from your presence?" (Psalm 139:7)*

God Is All-Knowing

He sees what you cannot. He knows what you do not. His wisdom is perfect and without limit.

> *"Great is our Lord and mighty in power; his understanding has no limit." (Psalm 147:5)*

God Is Unchanging

In a shifting, unpredictable world, He remains our anchor.

> *"I the Lord do not change. So you, the descendants of Jacob, are not destroyed." (Malachi 3:6)*

God Is Gracious

He gives what we could never earn. His grace lifts, empowers, and restores.

> *"For it is by grace you have been saved, through faith—it is the gift of God." (Ephesians 2:8)*

God Is Merciful

He meets us not with condemnation but with compassion.

> *"The Lord is compassionate and gracious, slow to anger, abounding in love." (Psalm 103:8)*

God Is Faithful

He keeps every promise. He stands with us in every season.

> *"Know therefore that the Lord your God is God... keeping his covenant of love to a thousand generations." (Deuteronomy 7:9)*

Living a Faith-Filled Life

The more we know this God, the God of love, power, mercy, and truth, the more naturally faith flows from our lives. Faith isn't a feeling; it's a decision to trust the unshakable nature of God, regardless of what we see.

When you walk in faith, you align your life with Heaven's perspective. You don't just believe for the miraculous, you begin to live in the expectation of it.

So today, choose to believe again.

Speak boldly, because your words have power.

Pray with authority, because your faith activates Heaven.

Live surrendered, because God works through yielded vessels.

~✥~

The Power of a Profession of Faith

A Glorious Vision: Heaven Unveiled Through Faith

Imagine, if you will, standing not just before gates, but on the very threshold of eternity, where time kneels before glory and the atmosphere itself vibrates with sacred anticipation. Before you rise celestial gates, not made of mere metal, but woven from rivers of living gold, flowing upward like molten sunlight frozen mid-motion. They tower like mountains, carved with heavenly symbols no human tongue can utter, inlaid with every jewel not found in any earthly mine, sapphires the color of God's voice, emeralds that shimmer with mercy, and diamonds pulsing with the rhythm of divine love.

These gates breathe, they are alive, whispering eternity in waves of pure, luminous energy. Light cascades from them in fluid strands, wrapping around you like silk spun from starlight. The air carries a fragrance no flower could release: the scent of original creation, the aroma of a world untouched by sin, a breath of Eden itself. It is the smell of life as God always intended it to be.

You are not alone. All around you, creation seems to pause, watching. Above, a cathedral sky stretches beyond imagination, embroidered with galaxies that swirl in reverence. And from it descends a symphony of angelic voices, thundering with perfect unity, each note woven with light, power, and praise:

> *"Holy, Holy, Holy is the Lord God Almighty, who was, and is, and is to come!"*

Every word shakes your soul, not in fear, but in recognition. You are hearing the sound your spirit was created for, the eternal anthem of the King of Kings.

Then, it happens. You feel Him.

Not from afar, not hidden in mystery, but here, near, now. A Presence more real than anything you've ever touched. It moves toward you, not in haste, but in majesty. You feel it before you see it: the blazing, holy nearness of God Himself. His gaze is not distant, but direct. Not judging, but knowing. And in that gaze, your entire life is laid bare, yet instead of shame, you are overcome with welcome.

Every fear evaporates. Every doubt is stilled. Every regret fades like shadows under the noonday sun.

And in their place?

Peace, not a quiet moment, but a flood, a holy stillness that fills every crevice of your soul.

Love, not a concept, but a force that wraps around you, pours into you, becomes you.

Joy, so intense it breaks you open, and from your spirit erupts both laughter and tears, as if your very being has remembered something it long forgot.

Then you speak, not timidly, but with holy fire in your chest:

"I believe, Lord."

The instant the words leave your lips, eternity roars in response.

The gates do not merely open, they explode with glory, parting like a veil between mortality and majesty. From within pours a radiance that cannot be described, a river of living light, golden and silver and white-hot with the presence of the Almighty. It surges around you and invites you in, not as a guest, but as a child returning home.

And you step forward.

Not because you must, but because you were always meant to.

The ground beneath your feet glows with welcome. Colors you've never seen dance in the air. Every step you take is met with joy that comes not from around you, but from Heaven itself celebrating your arrival.

"Well done," a voice says, not thunderous, but intimate. It is God's voice, speaking not to the crowd, but to you.

In that moment, you are not just saved.

You are known.

You are wanted.

You are home.

Welcomed not as a guest, but as a long-awaited child, you step into a realm where every breath is worship, every color sings its own hymn, and every tear has been lovingly wiped away by the very hand of God. The glory in the air is both weightless and all-encompassing. Here, the promises are not just fulfilled, they are alive.

Faith is no longer the evidence of things hoped for, it is the vision of things seen.

And that glimpse becomes an everlasting reality.

This moment, the moment you said, "I believe", is not just emotional; it's eternal. A profession of faith is not simply words spoken aloud. It is the moment heaven rejoices, sins are forgiven, and eternal life begins.

Faith is the portal between earth and heaven, a bridge between brokenness and wholeness, despair and glory. It is the divine key that opens your life to God's transforming power.

But what exactly is a profession of faith? Why does it carry such eternal significance?

Let's journey deeper.

What Is a Profession of Faith?

A profession of faith is more than belief. It is a declaration of trust in Jesus Christ as Savior and Lord. It marks the beginning of your walk with God, the moment you step from darkness into light, from death into life.

> *Acts 16:31 — "Believe in the Lord Jesus, and you will be saved—you and your household."*

> *John 3:16 — "For God so loved the world, that He gave His only Son, that whoever believes in Him should not perish but have eternal life."*

In this declaration, "I trust in Jesus", you don't merely join a religion; you enter into a relationship. Heaven responds with salvation. And your soul begins a journey of everlasting change.

Why Is It So Powerful?

1. Jesus: The Source of Salvation

Only Jesus can offer salvation. He lived sinlessly, died sacrificially, and rose victoriously. In Him, we are reconciled to God and granted eternal life.

> Romans 10:9 — "If you declare with your mouth, 'Jesus is Lord,' and believe in your heart that God raised Him from the dead, you will be saved."

> John 14:6 — "I am the way, the truth, and the life. No one comes to the Father except through me."

2. Faith: The Bridge Between Now and Eternity

Faith connects what we hope for to what God has promised. Even when we cannot see, faith assures us that what we believe is real and coming.

> Hebrews 11:1 — "Now faith is the assurance of things hoped for, the conviction of things not seen."

3. Heaven Responds

Your profession of faith is not a private event, it is a cosmic celebration.

> Luke 15:7 — "There is joy in heaven over one sinner who repents."

Profession of Faith vs. Baptism

Though closely connected, these are distinct steps:

➢ Profession of Faith: A personal declaration of belief in Jesus. It marks your entry into salvation.

➢ Baptism: A public demonstration of your new identity in Christ. It symbolizes dying to your old self and being raised with Him.

Acts 10:44–48 — Cornelius believed, then was baptized—showing that belief always comes first, and baptism confirms it.

Three Lasting Truths About Faith

1. Faith Is Personal, Yet Public

Faith begins in the heart but doesn't stay hidden. It is a private surrender that results in a public declaration.

2. Faith Is Ongoing

Hebrews 10:23 — "Let us hold fast the confession of our hope without wavering, for He who promised is faithful."

Faith is not a one-time prayer, it is a lifetime of trust, obedience, and transformation.

3. Faith Unlocks God's Power

Ephesians 2:8–9 — "For it is by grace you have been saved, through faith... not by works."

God works through faith, not human effort. Through it, we are empowered to live in His strength.

Scripture That Affirms the Power of Faith

- 2 Corinthians 5:17 — "If anyone is in Christ, he is a new creation."
- Romans 5:1 — "Since we have been justified through faith, we have peace with God."
- John 10:9 — "I am the door. If anyone enters by me, he will be saved."

Conclusion: Faith Unlocks Heaven

A profession of faith is not just a decision. It is a divine turning point, a moment where eternity intersects time, and your soul begins its true journey.

It is the key that unlocks the power of heaven in your life, the day you step into promise, hope, love, and purpose.

Heaven is ready.

The gates stand open.

Will you step forward and declare your trust in Jesus today?

Prayer: Embracing the Power of Faith

Heavenly Father,

Thank You for the gift of faith that opens the door to Your kingdom and transforms our lives. I declare my trust in You, Lord Jesus, as my Savior and Redeemer. Strengthen my faith to hold fast to Your promises, even in the face of trials. Help me to live as a testimony of Your grace and power, drawing others to experience the joy of salvation.

May my profession of faith be more than words, let it be a life transformed by Your love and guided by Your Spirit. Open the portals of heaven in my life, Lord, and pour out Your blessings, peace, and purpose.

In the mighty name of Jesus, I pray. Amen.

"Faith doesn't expire in the storm, it endures, conquers, and declares, 'I am more than a conqueror through Him who loves me.'"

"In all these things we are more than conquerors through him who loved us."
— Romans 8:37 (NIV)

Chapter 15

LIVING AS AN OVERCOMER IN EVERY SEASON

Life is a journey filled with both triumphs and trials. But through faith in God, we are empowered to rise above every challenge and walk in unshakable victory. Faith is more than belief , it is a spiritual catalyst that activates heaven's authority in our daily battles.

What gives faith this power? It is not rooted in human optimism but in divine reality. Faith connects us to the limitless power of God, made available through the death and resurrection of Jesus Christ. As Romans 10:9 declares, "If you confess with your mouth, 'Jesus is Lord,' and believe in your heart that God raised Him from the dead, you will be saved." If we can believe in the miracle of Christ's resurrection, what circumstance can we not entrust to God?

Faith enables us to continually draw from God's ever-present power. Hebrews 11:6 reminds us, "Without faith it is impossible to please God, because anyone who comes to Him must believe that He exists and that He rewards those who earnestly seek Him." If faith pleases God and brings His reward, what does that reward look like in the midst of hardship?

Paul gives us the answer: "In all these things we are more than conquerors through Him who loved us" (Romans 8:37). Faith fuels our perseverance, sustains our hope, and transforms impossible situations into divine opportunities for God's glory. Victory is not only possible; it is assured for those who trust in the power of the risen Christ.

Transformative faith is not passive. It equips us to overcome life's trials, resist spiritual opposition, and stand firm in God's promises. Through faith, we gain full access to God's authority, enabling us to live as overcomers in every season. It shields us in spiritual warfare and sustains us through daily challenges.

The Apostle John declares, "For everyone born of God overcomes the world. This is the victory that has overcome the world, even our faith. Who is it that overcomes the world? Only the one who believes that Jesus is the Son of God" (1 John 5:4–5). Faith in Christ is the key to victory because it connects us to the One who has already conquered sin, death, and the enemy.

This kind of faith empowers us to face every challenge with confidence, knowing that God's promises never fail. We can declare victory, not because of our strength, but because of His authority working through us.

Paul describes faith as a shield that protects us in spiritual warfare. In Ephesians 6:16, he writes, "Take up the shield of faith, with which you can extinguish all the flaming arrows of the evil one." The enemy's attacks often come in the form of fear, doubt, or lies meant to weaken our trust in God. But faith serves as our defense, keeping us grounded in truth.

For example:

➢ Fear: Faith reminds us that "God has not given us a spirit of fear but of power, love, and a sound mind" (2 Timothy 1:7).

➢ Doubt: Faith clings to God's promises even when circumstances say otherwise. Like the psalmist, we declare, "When I am afraid, I put my trust in you" (Psalm 56:3).

➢ Discouragement: Faith recalls God's faithfulness and His power to work all things for our good (Romans 8:28).

By standing firm in faith, we not only resist the enemy's attacks but also claim victory over every spiritual battle that comes against us.

Victory through faith is not a one-time event, it's a daily posture of confidence in God's power. Even when opposition arises, faith equips us to persevere and thrive.

Just like David, today's believer might face a financial crisis, a terminal diagnosis, or betrayal, yet faith declares, "The battle is the Lord's." David's victory wasn't just about defeating a giant; it was about his unwavering trust in God's ability to deliver. While others saw an impossible fight, David remembered, "The Lord who rescued me from the paw of the lion and the paw of the bear will rescue me from the hand of this Philistine" (1 Samuel 17:37).

David's faith transformed the battlefield. In the same way, our faith allows us to see life's giants as opportunities for God to demonstrate His supernatural power through us.

Every believer has access to this overcoming faith. So today — stand firm, speak God's promises, and live as more than a conqueror. Victory is not just a hope; it's your heritage through Christ.

We can live in daily victory by:

> - **Remembering Past Victories:** Reflecting on how God has worked in our lives strengthens our confidence for present battles.

> - **Speaking in Faith:** Declaring God's promises over our circumstances reinforces our trust in Him.

> - **Staying Rooted in Worship:** Praising God in the midst of trials shifts our focus from the problem to His sovereignty.

One of the most powerful ways to live as an overcomer is to celebrate and share the victories God has given you. Testimonies inspire faith in others and remind us of God's faithfulness.

> - **The Power of Testimony:** Revelation 12:11 declares, *"They triumphed over him by the blood of the Lamb and by the word of their testimony."* Sharing your story of faith and victory silences the enemy's lies and strengthens the faith of those who hear it.

➢ **Encouraging Others:** Your testimony might be the encouragement someone needs to keep believing for their breakthrough. Whether it's a story of healing, provision, or spiritual deliverance, your victories reflect God's transformative power.

➢ **Gratitude for God's Faithfulness**: Testimonies help us remain grateful for what God has done, building our faith for future challenges.

Victory Through Faith: Living as an Overcomer in Every Season

As we come to this chapter's conclusion, victory through faith is the hallmark of a life transformed by God's power and authority. It equips us to face spiritual battles, overcome daily challenges, and walk confidently in the promises of God.

Like David, we can stand before life's giants with the assurance that God fights for us. Like Paul, we can declare that we are "more than conquerors through Him who loved us" (Romans 8:37). And like countless believers throughout history, we can testify to the transformative power of faith that brings lasting change.

Faith doesn't avoid the battle, it transforms it. It equips us not just to survive, but to overcome with purpose and divine strength. So trust in God, wield the shield of faith, and live as an overcomer in every season. Victory is yours because of the One who has already overcome.

Faith reshapes our inner world so that we can influence the outer world. When we stand firm in God's promises and live yielded to His Word, we reflect His power and authority in every aspect of our lives.

~❖~

Walking in God's Power and Authority by Faith

Faith is not just belief, it is surrender. It's the doorway through which God releases His supernatural power and authority into our lives. When we operate in faith, we're not just enduring, we're partnering with Heaven to see the impossible become reality.

True faith says, "God, not my will, but Yours be done." It's a spiritual key that unlocks divine movement on earth.

You're Going Through Something, But Faith Has a Voice

And yet, faith is not just for theological discussion or lofty ideas, it speaks in the middle of your storm. If you're walking through grief, confusion, frustration, or transition, know this: faith still speaks.

And it speaks louder than your fear, louder than your pain, and louder than your doubt.

Faith says:

God is not just a way; He is The Way.

He's not part of your solution; He is the solution.

Not only does He know what you're facing, He has everything you need to overcome it. There is no deficit in God. He is not just enough; He is more than enough.

> *"But my God shall supply all your needs according to His riches in glory by Christ Jesus."*
> *—Philippians 4:19 (KJV)*

When you walk by faith, you're not begging for scraps from the devil's table, you're stepping into alignment with the abundance of Heaven. Faith declares:

"God had the answer before I ever saw the problem."

But more than solutions, God releases His will into your situation. And when His will enters, things shift. The atmosphere changes. You

are no longer driven by fear or personal agenda; you are transformed by His will and empowered to walk in it.

God's Power and Authority Are Connected to His Promises

Every promise of God is backed by His power and enforced by His authority. His promises aren't suggestions; they are divine decrees that carry the full weight of Heaven.

> *"God is not a man, that He should lie; neither the son of man, that He should repent. Hath He said, and shall He not do it?"*
> —Numbers 23:19 (KJV)

When God speaks, His words carry both the ability to bring something into existence and the right to rule over every opposition. That's authority.

So when you trust His promises, you're declaring:

"What God says about my situation is more powerful than what I see."

That is the essence of faith. And that kind of faith unlocks divine realities in your life.

What Faith in God Activates in Your Life

Faith doesn't manipulate God into action, it positions you to receive what He's already prepared.

Here's what faith activates:

1. Divine Power

The strength to overcome what would normally break you.

> *"You will receive power when the Holy Spirit has come upon you..."*
> —Acts 1:8

2. Divine Wisdom

Clarity in chaos — to make God-aligned decisions even when everything seems uncertain.

> *"If any of you lacks wisdom, let him ask of God... and it will be given."* —James 1:5

3. Divine Peace

A peace that doesn't make sense to the world but anchors you in the storm.

> *"The peace of God, which surpasses all understanding, will guard your hearts and minds..."* —Philippians 4:7

4. Divine Provision

More than finances, it's strength, opportunity, relationships, and everything needed to fulfill your purpose.

> *"The Lord is my Shepherd; I shall not want."* —Psalm 23:1

5. Divine Transformation

You're not just surviving trials; you're becoming more like Jesus through them.

> *"Be transformed by the renewing of your mind..."* —Romans 12:2

6. God's Grace and Mercy

Unmerited favor and divine compassion that lift you when you fall and carry you when you're weak.

> *"Let us then approach God's throne of grace with confidence... to receive mercy and find grace to help us in our time of need."* —Hebrews 4:16

God's grace empowers you beyond your limitations. His mercy lifts you when you fall. Together, they carry you through every valley.

Faith Transforms the Inner World to Influence the Outer World

Faith is not only about external victory, it's about internal alignment. When faith shapes your heart, it changes how you think, speak, act, and respond.

God uses faith to mold your inner life, your trust, your thoughts, your expectations, so He can release His outer will through your hands.

The more your inner world aligns with His Word, the more His power flows through you.

The Power of a Yielded Life

God doesn't just want to improve your life — He wants to transform you into who He created you to be in Christ.

He wants to:

➢ Align your life with His perfect will

➢ Shape your character with His nature

➢ Fill your days with His presence

➢ Empower your voice with His authority

➢ Use your testimony as a weapon against darkness

His promises are waiting.

His power is available.

His authority is real.

But it all begins with one powerful word: "I yield."

You're not just going through something — you're being led through something by the God who never fails.

So Rise in Faith. Surrender in Faith. Move Forward in Faith.

Because when you yield your life to God:

➢ His will is released,

➢ His promises come alive,

➢ And His power becomes your reality.

> *"Now to Him who is able to do exceedingly, abundantly above all that we ask or think, according to the power that works in us..."*
> *—Ephesians 3:20 (NKJV)*

Your faith makes room for the miraculous.

Your surrender unlocks Heaven's best.

And your life? It's about to become a testimony of faith that transforms, God's power and authority fully unlocked.

My Final Words for You

Faith That Transforms: God's Power and Authority Unlocked

As we bring this journey of faith to a close, I pray the truths revealed in these pages have stirred a passion in your heart, a hunger to walk in the fullness of God's promises. Faith is not passive belief or an abstract concept. It is a living response to God's Word, a divine connection that unleashes His power and authority to transform your life from the inside out.

From the very beginning, faith has been central to God's design. "By faith we understand that the universe was formed at God's command..." (Hebrews 11:3). Faith is not new to God, it is the eternal language of His kingdom, the force by which He brings His will to pass. What may feel uncertain to us is already settled in Him.

Now, you stand equipped with more than head knowledge, you hold the spiritual key that bridges heaven and earth. Faith moves

mountains, redefines circumstances, and positions you to walk in God-given authority.

Faith connects you to God's unlimited power and opens the door to divine intervention. When you operate in faith, you are no longer confined by natural limitations. Instead, you align with God's sovereign power, allowing Him to work through you in extraordinary ways.

Jesus said, "Everything is possible for one who believes." (Mark 9:23). This isn't motivational hype, it's a spiritual law. When faith is present, impossibilities bow. The authority of God is released to heal, restore, and provide. Faith is the vehicle through which His promises manifest in your life.

Imagine a life where peace surpasses your understanding, where joy becomes your strength, and where love overflows from you to those around you. That's not just poetic, it's the fruit of faith fully embraced.

As your intimacy with God deepens, faith becomes the natural overflow of your walk with Him. It's not rooted in emotions or changing circumstances — but in the unchanging truth of His Word. Faith is trust in its purest form, a surrender to God's wisdom, love, and power. When you walk in faith, you partner with God to release His will on the earth.

This is not a passive relationship, it's a divine collaboration. Through faith, you can declare healing, speak life into dead situations, and release God's peace and provision into every area of your life.

God wants you to walk in victory. He stands with you, fights for you, and redeems every setback for your good. "If God is for us, who can be against us?" (Romans 8:31). He is not only your protector but your strategist, intercepting every fiery dart meant for harm and turning it into fuel for your destiny.

Heavenly Father,

As I complete this journey on Faith That Transforms, I thank You with a heart full of gratitude. Thank You for being my guide, my strength in weakness, and my hope in every trial. You've shown me that faith is the currency of heaven, the way Your power and authority are released into my life.

Fill me with Your peace. Restore my spirit. Let Your love shine through every circumstance I face. May I continue to trust Your perfect plan and celebrate every victory You bring, knowing You are for me and fighting on my behalf.

In Jesus's mighty name,

Amen.

About the Author

Anthony Vaughn is a devoted servant of God, dynamic teacher, speaker, and ordained servant leader with a passion for unlocking the power of faith in the lives of believers. His unique ability to break down Scripture with clarity, revelation, and practical insight makes his writing a transformative experience for those seeking to deepen their relationship with God.

With an inspirational and thought-provoking approach, Anthony challenges the mind, stirs the heart, and ignites the spirit. He encourages readers to think deeply, explore hidden truths, and embrace the profound wisdom found in God's Word. His teachings are not just about knowledge, but about spiritual awakening, illuminating fresh perspectives and guiding believers toward a life of purpose, faith, and divine understanding.

Anthony Vaughn's writing is infused with wisdom, offering fresh revelations that bring the promises, power, and grace of God into clearer focus. He leads readers beyond the surface of Scripture into the inner courtyard of God's presence, where faith is strengthened, hearts are renewed, and lives are transformed. Whether through his writings, teachings, or speaking engagements, Anthony Vaughn is committed to equipping believers with the tools to walk boldly in their faith, discover their divine calling, and experience the fullness of God's love.

To learn more about Anthony's work or to connect for speaking engagements, visit www.anthonyvaughnbooks.com